TRACKS

about 2¼"

GRAY SQUIRREL

LEFT HIND FOOT

LEFT FORE FOOT

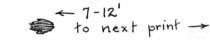

← 7-12'
to next print →

about 2¾" JACK RABBIT

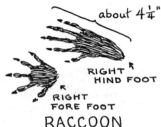

about 4¼"

RIGHT HIND FOOT

RIGHT FORE FOOT

RACCOON

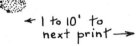

about 6"

← 1 to 10' to
next print →

SNOWSHOE HARE

about 2"

LEFT FORE FOOT

LEFT HIND FOOT

MARTEN

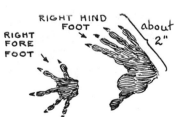

RIGHT HIND FOOT

about 2"

RIGHT FORE FOOT

OPOSSUM

about 2½"

HIND FOOT

COYOTE

about 3"

LEFT FORE FOOT

LEFT HIND FOOT

FISHER

about 1¾"

HIND FOOT

RED FOX

RIGHT HIND FOOT

RIGHT FORE FOOT

about 2"

MINK

TRACKS

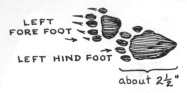

LEFT
FORE FOOT →

LEFT HIND FOOT →

about 2½"

STRIPED SKUNK

about 2"

BOBCAT

LEFT FORE
FOOT →

about 5"

← LEFT
HIND FOOT

WOLVERINE

about 4"

RIGHT HIND
FOOT

RIGHT
FORE
FOOT

MOUNTAIN LION

RIGHT
HIND
FOOT

RIGHT
FORE
FOOT

← about 12"
between
tracks

about 9"

BLACK BEAR

about 3"

← about 20" →
between tracks

RIGHT
HIND
FOOT

RIGHT
FORE FOOT

MULE DEER

← about 15" →
between
tracks

about 3"

BIGHORN SHEEP

QUAIL - walking

- hopping

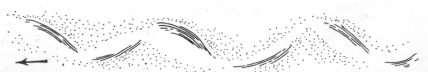

PACIFIC RATTLESNAKE

Volume 2 of the American Wildlife Region Series

THE SIERRA NEVADAN
WILDLIFE REGION

Revised and Enlarged Edition

By Vinson Brown, M. A.

and

Robert Livezey, Ph. D.
Professor of Zoology at
Sacramento State College

MAJOR ILLUSTRATORS

Plants: Charles Yocom, Emily Reid
Mammals and Birds: Jerry Buzzell, Iain Baxter
Reptiles and Amphibians: Robert Stebbins
Fish: Carol Lyness, Emily Reid

Cover Picture Courtesy of J. Carroll Reiners

Copyright © 1962, Naturegraph Co.
Pictures with IB Copyright 1961 by Iain Baxter

Paper Edition ISBN 0-911010-02-5
Cloth Edition ISBN 0-911010-03-3

TABLE OF CONTENTS

Published by Naturegraph Co., Healdsburg, California

ABOUT THE REGION

This book is the second of a series on the wildlife regions of America. Wildlife regions, such as the Sierra Nevadan Wildlife Region (shown on map), are distinctive natural geographic areas of similar climate and topography, which tend to have certain typical animals and plants within their boundaries. There is, however, much overlapping between wildlife regions (as shown by overlap with Cascade Region illustrated on map) so that their boundaries should never be considered as rigid lines.

THE SIERRA NEVADAN WILDLIFE REGION

Area of Overlap with the Cascade Wildlife Region

Life zones of the region are shown in the profile of the mountains that appears below.

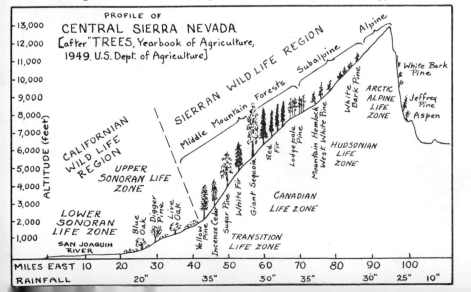

PROFILE OF CENTRAL SIERRA NEVADA [after "TREES, Yearbook of Agriculture, 1949. U.S. Dept. of Agriculture]

SIERRAN WILD LIFE REGION

CALIFORNIAN WILD LIFE REGION

UPPER SONORAN LIFE ZONE

LOWER SONORAN LIFE ZONE

SAN JOAQUIN RIVER

Blue Oak · Digger Pine · Live Oak · Yellow Pine · Incense Cedar · Sugar Pine · White Fir · Giant Sequoia · Red Fir · Lodgepole Pine · Mountain Hemlock · West. White Pine · White Bark Pine · White Bark Pine · Jeffrey Pine · Aspen

Middle Mountain Forests · Subalpine · Alpine

ARCTIC ALPINE LIFE ZONE

HUDSONIAN LIFE ZONE

CANADIAN LIFE ZONE

TRANSITION LIFE ZONE

MILES EAST 10   20   30   40   50   60   70   80   90   100

RAINFALL   20"   35"   50"   35"   30"   25"   10"

The Transition Zone appears on the west slope with the beginning of the Ponderosa Pine Forest (page 13). The Canadian Zone includes the Red Fir Forest (page 13), and part of the Lodgepole Pine Forest (page 14). The Hudsonian Zone is the same as the Sub-alpine Forest (page 22), and the Arctic-Alpine Zone is the area of the Alpine Fell Fields and snowy peaks of the mountain tops (page 33).

HOW TO USE THIS BOOK

Since this book has been purposely kept small to make its selling price reasonable and so reach the widest possible number of users, only basic information is given about the animals and plants described. For more details, turn to the larger books listed on page 94.

This book provides a simple, easy introduction to the common wild animals and plants of the Sierra Nevadan Wildlife Region. Its main purpose is to show you how to learn about the animals and plants in relation to where they like to live. For example, if you are walking through a middle mountain meadow in the region and have this book along, it tells you in an easy way about the common animals and plants that surround you.

The first step to take is to make yourself familiar with the map of the Sierra Nevadan Wildlife Region on page 4, and with the profile of the mountains shown below it. Next you had best study the pictures and descriptions of the different habitats starting on page 9, so that you can recognize them on a hike or trip. Remember that naturally there is some variation in the appearance of these areas so that what you see will not always be exactly like the picture.

Let us suppose that you are taking a hike and you come into a Sub-alpine Forest, which you identify from the picture of such a forest on page 22. Beginning with this page, you will find descriptions and illustrations of the common plants of the Sub-alpine Forest. Look all about you. Study all the parts of the plants you see. Then, using the descriptions and pictures, begin to identify the plants described.

If no description of a geographical range appears with the name of a plant or animal, this means that it is found in most parts of the Sierra Nevadan Wildlife Region, as shown on the map on page 4. If, however, a description of the range is given, you can tell from this description whether the plant or animal is found in your neighborhood. For example, if you live in Weaverville, Trinity County, and find a plant or animal listed as appearing "from Tulare Co. north, but not in the north Coast Ranges," then you know the plant is not found in your neighborhood. If, on the contrary, the description says the plant is "found from Lake Co. and Fresno Co. north," then you know it is found in your locality because Weaverville is in the middle of the North Coast Ranges north of Lake County.

Because plants are more commonly found limited to certain wild-life areas or habitats, and so help to distinguish those areas, all the plant descriptions are grouped under the wildlife habitat sections. Thus, for example, all the "Sub-alpine Forest" plants are grouped together. Some plants that are found more commonly in other habitats, but are also found in the Sub-alpine Forest, are listed by name only at the end of the section, and the page number of each is given. Only very common plants are listed and described, but these probably include at least 90% of the individual plants noted in any given habitat or wildlife area.

Also at the end of each habitat section there is a list of the common animals that are found there. Opposite each animal's name is a page number where the description of the animal can be found. Because of the fact that animals are frequently found in many different kinds of wildlife habitats, their descriptions and pictures are placed together in the last half of the book, with one section on mammals, one on birds, another on reptiles, a fourth on amphibians, and a last section on fishes. At the head of each of these sections there is a brief introduction telling you how to use the section for identifying the animals. On the side of the page bordering each description appears a list of abbreviations giving habitats in which each species is found.

When walking in a meadow, for example, you suddenly see a bird whose name you would like to know. Turn to the bird section of the book and follow the directions given at the beginning of the section as to how to identify the bird, looking only at the birds that are found in meadows. For any other kind of animal, such as a mammal or reptile, turn to the proper section of the book and follow the instructions.

Another method to use is to turn to the meadow section of the book and go through the list of birds found there until you find the names of birds you think might include the one you are watching. Turn then to pages where descriptions and pictures of these birds are found and study them until you find the one you believe is right.

Since every description is numbered and the pictures also numbered, you can carefully study the pictures and learn to test yourself by naming them without looking at the names.

ABBREVIATIONS

" = inches; ' = feet; Fam. = Family; N. = north; S. = south; E. = east; W. = west. ♂ = male; ♀ = female. * = edible plants.

Str. Wd. = Streamside Woodland; Conif. = Middle Mountain Forests; Sub-alp. = Sub-alpine Forest; Mead. = Middle Mountain Meadows; Alp. = Alpine Fell Fields or Meadows; Rocks = Rocky Areas; Brush = Brushland Areas; Sage = Sagebrush Areas; Water = Fresh Water Areas; Pin-Jun. = Pinyon-Juniper Woodland; Bldg. = Buildings.

COMMON PLANTS AND HOW TO IDENTIFY THEM

There are certain immensely successful and numerous plants in each wildlife area that help to identify that area. Thus, there are the willows, dogwoods and maples in the streamside woodland; the manzanita, deer brush and whitethorn in the mountain brushland. This book helps you get acquainted just with these very common plants, which are the ones you are far the most likely to see.

The trouble is, because of the presence of less common plants, you may confuse one of them with one of the commoner kinds described in this book. That is why it is necessary for you to carefully follow the directions given below.

The pictures shown will help you understand the different kinds of flowers, flower formations, and leaves that are useful in identifying plants. Study these pictures carefully so you understand the meaning of the words used.

Each picture or figure in this section is numbered in numerical order from beginning to end. When you see one of these numbers in a description of a plant, turn to the correct figure in this section and you will find a helpful illustration of what the description tells about.

Besides the general pictures on plants, a number of separate pictures are shown near the plant descriptions. Use these also to help you with identifications. When you are studying a plant to determine its name, carefully look at every part of it: the leaves, the flowers, the fruit, the seeds, the bark and even the way the branches are formed. When you add all this knowledge together and compare what you have learned with the pictures and descriptions, you are soon likely to come up with the correct name.

The pictures shown here have been adapted from Don G. Kelley's drawings in THE AMATEUR NATURALIST'S HANDBOOK, by Vinson Brown, with kind permission of Little, Brown & Co. of Boston.

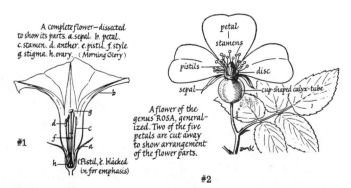

#1 and #2. Two typical flowers, showing the names of their parts.

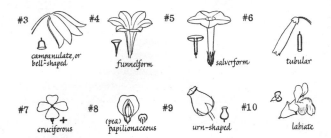

#3 to #10. **Types of Flowers:** #3 and #4 are <u>apetalous,</u> which means without distinct petals and sepals; #7 and #8 are <u>choripetalous,</u> which means the petals and sepals are each completely free from each other; #5, 6, 9 and 10 are <u>sympetalous,</u> which means the petals and sepals are all more or less closely joined together.

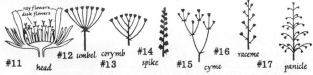

#11 to #17. **Types of flower formations.** The daisy and sun-flower look like single flowers, but really are heads of flowers (#11).

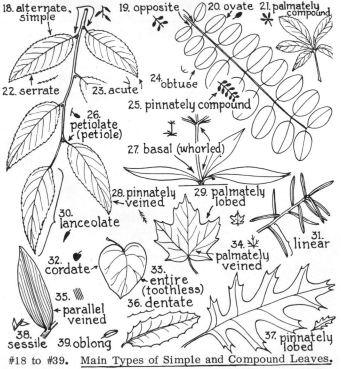

#18 to #39. **Main Types of Simple and Compound Leaves.**

THE STREAMSIDE WOODLAND

The streamside woodland is not so well-developed in the Sierra as it is down in the lowlands of the Californian Wildlife Region (see Volume 1 of this series). The higher one goes in the mountains the less the streamside woodland is distinct from the surrounding mountain forest, so that in the sub-alpine forest near the mountain tops there is little or no streamside woodland at all. Thus, this habitat is developed best in the lower part of the middle forest, particularly alongside the ponderosa pine forest (see page 13) where thick growths of willows, dogwoods, maples and other moisture-loving plants line the streams. Here is a favorite habitat of many birds who like a plentiful supply of water and also insect life.

1. SIERRA WATER FERN, Lastrea oregana; Polypodiaceae, Fern Fam. 1-3' high; in the form of tufts with very short stalks (1-2"); the fronds membrane-like and deeply pinnately lobed (#25). From Tuolumne and Trinity Counties north, 3000-5000' altitude. — Str. Wd. Conif.

2. LADY FERN, Athyrium filix-femina. 2-4' high, forming large clumps; fronds 1-2 1/2' long, 6-11" wide, pinnately-lobed (#37) very deeply, and with the lobes toothed at their tips. From Trinity Co. and southern California Mts. north. — Str.Wd. Mead. Conif. Sub-alp.

3. FIVE-FINGER FERN, Adiantum pedatum. 4-16" high, with very distinctive finger-shaped fronds, palmately-lobed (#29). Up to 11,000' in altitude, from San Gabriel Mts. north. (Not illustrated.) — Str. Wd. Rocks Conif.

4. SMALL TIGER LILY, Lilium parvum; Liliaceae, Lily Fam. 1-7' high. Flowers 1-1 1/4" long and spotted purple on yellow-orange. Long, narrow, light-green leaves. Usually found above 6000'. — Str.Wd. Mead. Sub-alp.

5. LEOPARD LILY, Lilium pardalinum. Flowers yellow (rarely red or dark red) with orange-red or purple spots. Forms large colonies along streams below 6000' altitude. Plant 1 1/2-4' high. — Str. Wd.

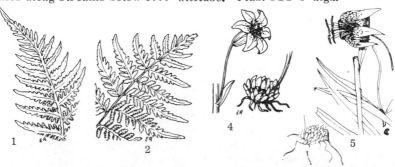

1   2   4   5

WILLOWS (Salix species; Salicaceae, Willow and Poplar Fam.).
Willows are difficult to tell separately, even by experts. 3-30' high;
leaves mainly light green in color, linear (#31) to oblong (#39) in
shape and with entire or smooth (#33) edges.
The yellow ♂ (S = staminate) and green ♀ (P =
pistillate) flowers are in distinctive catkins
as is shown. 5 common willows are described below.

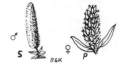

Str.Wd.
Mead.
6. EASTWOOD'S WILLOW, Salix eastwoodiae. A shrub, 3-6'
high, with dark, hairy twigs; stamens gray-hairy. From Tulare Co.
north (except in North Coast Ranges), usually above 6000'.

Str.Wd.
Mead.
7. SIERRA WILLOW, Salix orestera. 3-9' shrub. Leaves silky &
sharp-pointed at both ends. Not in N. Coast Ranges; usually 7000' +.

Str.Wd.
Mead.
8. LEMMON'S WILLOW, Salix lemmoni. 3-16' shrub. Leaves
shining deep green above; young twigs yellowish; mostly above 6000'.

Str.Wd.
Mead.
Conif.
9. SCOULER'S WILLOW, Salix scouleriana. 12-30' tree. The
commonest willow of middle forest streams; very variable in leaf
shape, etc.; young leaves and bark have bad odor. Below 10,000'.

Str.Wd.
Mead.
Conif.
10. GEYER'S WILLOW, Salix geyeriana. 3-15' tall shrub or tree.
Twigs black with a bluish tinge; very small leaves for a willow.

Str.Wd.
Conif.
Mead.
11. QUAKING ASPEN, Populus tremuloides. 6-25' tall; graceful and slender tree, with smooth, greenish-white bark; light green
leaves always trembling in the breeze. From Tulare Co. north.

Str.Wd.
Conif.
12. MOUNTAIN DOGWOOD, Cornus nuttallii; Cornaceae, Dogwood Fam. 10-45' tall tree; the large, white or reddish-tinged flower heads (#11) are 1/2-1" wide and look like flowers, but are actually
made up of many tiny flowers surrounded by petal-like bracts. The
cherry-like fruits are very tiny and bright red-colored. Green twigs
turn dark red to almost black with age; leaves 2-5" long.

Str.Wd.
Conif.
13A. BIG LEAF MAPLE, Acer macrophyllum; Aceraceae, Maple
Fam. Wide-topped tree of 25-90', with palmate (#34) leaves; tiny
flowers in racemes (#16); 2-winged seeds. B. MOUNTAIN MAPLE,

Str.Wd.
Conif.
Acer glabrum, has smaller, more compact, tooth-edged leaves, and
the seeds have wings at right angles. C. VINE MAPLE, A. circina-
tum. Vine-like, with leaves similar to A. glabrum, but even-lobed.

Str.Wd.
Mead.
Conif.
14. BOX ELDER, Acer negundo. 18-60' tall, round-headed tree.
Leaves pinnately 3-lobed, sometimes 5-lobed; ovate and coarsely
serrate (toothed), densely furry beneath; seeds red, turning yellow.

Str.Wd.
Conif.
15. WESTERN AZALEA, Rhododendron occidentale; Ericaceae,
Heath Fam. 3-14' high shrub, with 1-4" long, usually smooth leaves;
beautiful, showy, white or pinkish flowers, 1 1/2-2" long, with one
petal usually splotched with yellow; bark shreddy; 1-winged seed.

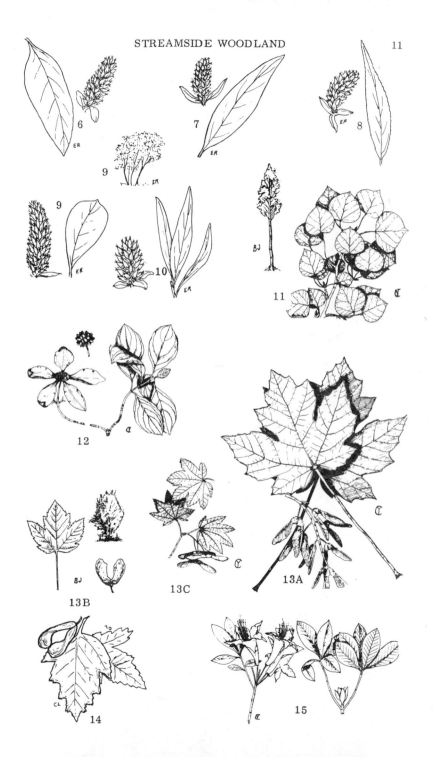

Other Plants Found in the Streamside Woodland

Sword Fern, 14
Brake Fern, 15
Malpais Blue Grass, 27
Red Fescue Grass, 27
Sedges, 27

Corn Lily, 28
Blue-eyed Grass, 28
West. Dog Violet, 30
Giant Hyssop, 30

Thimbleberry, 18
Currant, 18
Indian Paint Brush, 30
Monkey Flower, 30

Common Animals of the Streamside Woodland

Mammals
Virginia Opossum, 41
Broad-footed Mole, 41
Shrew Mole, 42
Vagrant Shrew, 42
Adorned Shrew, 42
Yosemite Shrew, 42
Dusky Shrew, , 42
Water Shrew, 42

Little Brown Ba 42
California Myotis, 42
Long-eared Myotis, 42
Small-footed Myotis, 44
Hairy-winged Myotis, 44
Red Bat, 44
Big Brown Bat, 44
Hoary Bat, 44
Silvery-haired Bat, 44

Black Bear, 45
Raccoon, 45
Ring-tailed Cat, 45
Mink, 45
Long-tailed Weasel, 46
River Otter, 46
Striped Skunk, 46
Spotted Skunk, 46
Grey Fox, 46
Coyote, 46

Calif. Ground Squirrel, 48
Gray Squirrel, 50
Beaver, 50
White-footed Mouse, 50
Pinyon Mouse, 50
W. Harvest Mouse, 52
Dusky-footed Woodrat, 52
Pacific Jumping Mouse, 52
Norway Rat, 53
Mountain Beaver, 54
Porcupine, 54

Snowshoe Hare, 54

Mule Deer, 55
Elk, 55

Birds
Great Blue Heron, 57
Wood Duck, 58

Cooper's Hawk, 59
Red-tailed Hawk, 60
Sparrow Hawk, 60
Mourning Dove, 60
Killdeer, 62
Common Snipe, 62
Spotted Sandpiper, 62
Horned Owl, 63

Belted Kingfisher, 65
Red-shafted Flicker, 65
Hairy Woodpecker, 66
Downy Woodpecker, 66
Red-breasted Sapsucker, 66
Tree Swallow, 67
Western Flycatcher, 67
Traill's Flycatcher, 67
W. Wood Pewee, 67

Steller's Jay, 68
Crow, 68
Black-billed Magpie, 68
Bush-tit, 69
House Wren, 70

Robin, 71
Russet-backed Thrush, 72
Western Bluebird, 72

Warbling Vireo, 73
Solitary Vireo, 73
Orange-crowned Warbler, 74
Yellow Warbler, 74
Macgillivray's Warbler, 75

Wilson's Warbler, 75

Brewer's Blackbird, 75
Bullock's Oriole, 75

Black-headed Grosbeak, 76
Lesser Goldfinch, 77
Lazuli Bunting, 78
Purple Finch, 76
Fox Sparrow, 78

Reptiles
Northern Alligator Lizard, 81
Rubber Boa, 82
Sharp-tailed Snake, 82
Common King Snake, 82
W. Ring-necked Snake, 82
Common Garter Snake, 84
Western Garter Snake, 84

Amphibians
Rough-skinned Newt, 85
California Newt, 85
Long-toed Salamander, 85
Pacific Giant Salamander, 86
Eschscholtz's Salamander, 86
Black Salamander, 87
Western Toad, 87
Pacific Tree-frog, 87
Yellow-legged Frog, 87
Red-legged Frog, 88

Leopard Frog, 88

THE MIDDLE MOUNTAIN FORESTS

Typical Ponderosa Pine Forest; photo by U. S. Forest Service.

If you will turn back to the Profile of the Sierra Nevada Mountains on page 4, you will see that there is a stretch of thick forest on the mountainside extending from the beginning of the ponderosa pine forest up to the lodgepole forest, between about 3000 and 8250 feet in the central Sierra. There is a similar, though narrower, stretch of forest on the east side of the mountains. Though this forest includes both the Transition and Canadian Life Zones and is actually made up of several types of forests, it furnishes a fairly similar habitat for most animal life, and so is grouped together here under the title "Middle Mountain Forests." Many animals, particularly birds, come into the lower part of this forest in early summer, and gradually move higher as the season gets warmer. Three different main types of forest are found here, each dominated and identified by one dominant kind of tree. Many of the plants that are most common in one of the three types of forest are found less commonly in the others.

a. Ponderosa Pine Forest (illustrated at top of this page.) This is the lowest coniferous forest of the mountainside, found from 1200-5500 feet in the Mt. Shasta region, 3000-6000 feet in the north Coast Ranges, 2500-6000 feet in the central Sierra, and 5000-8000 feet in the mountains of southern California. It is a typical Transition Zone forest, fairly open and with little undergrowth. Precipitation runs from 25-80" a year; frost-free days about 90-120; temperature in summer reaches about 80-90 degrees; in winter it drops to 32 degrees or lower. The dominant plants are the ponderosa pine, the white fir, the incense cedar, the sugar pine and the black oak.

b. Red Fir Forest (illustrated at top of page 14). This is the dense, main forest of the Canadian Life Zone, but the red fir is commonest on the western slope of the Sierra, whereas the Jeffrey Pine is the common tree of this zone on the steeper east slope. The red fir forest appears just above the ponderosa pine forest on the west slope. The precipitation averages 35-65" a year, with very heavy snow; the summer temperature runs about 73-85 degrees at midday, but in winter drops to 26-16 degrees. There are 40-70 frost-free days.

Typical Red-fir Forest, photo courtesy U. S. Forest Service.

Typical Lodgepole Pine Forest, photo courtesy U.S. Forest Serv.

c. Lodgepole Pine Forest. Trees often close together, but interspersed with frequent meadows; found mainly above the red fir forest as an upper border of the Canadian Life Zone, and sometimes mixed with the lower border of the sub-alpine forest. Precipitation averages about 30-60", mostly snow; frost-free days about 40 or often less; summer temperatures reach 65-75 degrees; winter day time temperatures drop to about 18-10 degrees. Mainly from central Sierra north.

FERNS

16. SWORD FERN, Polystichum munitum; Polypodiaceae, Fern Fam. 1-5' high; evergreen fern, with the stalks covered with needle-shaped, brown scales; single long fronds appear in clumps; frond-lobes with ear-like bumps at base as shown. Usually on stony ground; common under Big Trees (Sequoia).

Conif.
Rocks
Str.Wd.

STIPES
WITH
PAPERY
SCALES

16.

‹17. COMMON BRAKE FERN, Pteridium aquilinum. 1-5' tall, with leaves erect or ascending, graceful; stem stout, generally solitary, with dark root-stocks that appear corded; fronds appear with tiny white hairs beneath.   Young shoots and rootstocks cooked by Indians. Common ground cover, especially under Ponderosa Pine.

Mead.
Conif.
Sub-alp.
Str.Wd.
Brush
Rocks

TREES

18. PONDEROSA PINE, Pinus ponderosa; Pinaceae, Pine Fam. 100-240' tall tree, evergreen. Short branches turn upwards at ends; crown spire-like or sometimes flat-topped in dry localities; needles in 3's, bright yellow green, making broom-like tufts on branch ends; bark in old trees forms yellowish-red picture puzzle like plates. There is a sweet, vanila-like odor to the fresh bark.

Conif.

19. JEFFREY PINE, Pinus jeffreyi. 90-190' tall; old bark usually splits into large, reddish-brown, irregular plates, but not as picture-puzzle-like as in the ponderosa pine; evergreen needles in 3's, dull blue-green in color; 4 1/2-6" long.   Young trees are best told from young ponderosa pines by the smell, which is much less pleasantly sweet, and by the cones being larger and the branchlets smoother. Common in dry places, especially E. side of Sierra.

Conif.
Sub-alp.

*20. SUGAR PINE, Pinus lambertiana. 150-260' tall, evergreen tree. The main branches are large and horizontal; branchlets covered with hair; old bark covered with loose reddish or purplish-brown scales; needles in 5's, very hard and sharp-pointed; the cones are enormously long; sap sweet, used for sugar by Indians.

Conif.

21. LODGEPOLE PINE, Pinus murrayana. 60-160' tall, evergreen, with usually a very straight trunk except where wind-swept; bark very thin and covered with loose scales; slender dark green needles are in 2's; 1-2" long cones are shining, reddish-brown.

Conif.
Sub-alp.

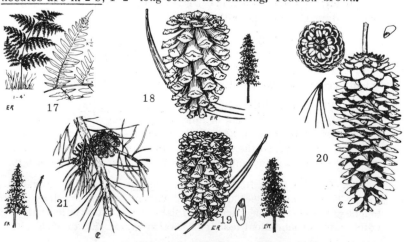

22. WESTERN or MOUNTAIN WHITE PINE, Pinus monticola. Evergreen, 9-160' high, slender tree, with narrow, symmetrical top when in dense forests; more open and loosely-branched in form when found in open forests; bark about 1" thick and divided into nearly square plates; needles in 5's, usually 2-4" long, bluish-green and marked with white lines; cones 4-8" long.

Conif. Sub-alp.

23. RED FIR, Abies magnifica. Up to 180-220' high, with short branches, lower ones drooping; the branchlets become silvery-gray the second year; the 4-sided, 2-ribbed needles are blue-green, 1-1 1/2" long, and very thick on the branchlets; tree appears spire-shaped.

Conif.

24. WHITE FIR, Abies concolor. Evergreen; may reach 200-260' high. The short, stout branches usually form a thin, spire-like top; has smooth and shining branchlets; the erect, pale blue-green needles are about 2-2 1/2" long and usually grooved; cones 2-4 1/2" long.

Conif.

25. DOUGLAS FIR, Pseudotsuga menziesii. An evergreen, up to 180-230' high; the lower branches usually droop, and all branches end in many drooping branchlets; old bark with broad ridges and deep grooves. Needles dark yellow or blue-green, 3/4 - 1 1/4" long, and pointing in all directions. From Fresno Co. north.

Conif.

26. MOUNTAIN HEMLOCK, Tsuga mertensiana. Evergreen; 75-160' high, with very slender, curved and drooping branches; branches often with up-curved tips; thick reddish-brown bark made up of rounded ridges with deep grooves between; needles light blue-green in color, and 1/2-3/4" long; cones 1-3" long. From Tulare Co. north.

Conif. Sub-alp.

27. GIANT SEQUOIA or BIG TREE, Sequoiadendron giganteum. Taxodiaceae, Taxodium Fam. An evergreen; 100-325' high; usually 80-220' up a straight column to the first branch, and 5-30' diameter to trunk; a deeply-grooved red bark; needles cling to the stems; most of the reddish-brown cones are 1 1/2-3' long. Forms thick groves, from Tulare Co. to Placer Co.

Conif.

28. INCENSE CEDAR, Libocedrus decurrens; Cupressaceae, Cypress Fam. An evergreen tree; up to 150-175' high, with very characteristic light green needles that cling to the branchlets; the bark is bright, reddish-brown and fiber-like; cones 3/4-1" long.

Conif.

*29. WESTERN JUNIPER, Juniperus occidentalis. Evergreen; 25-65' high, with very thick branches, spreading to form a flat top; reddish-brown bark about 3/5" thick; the greyish-green needles are in 3's, and close against the branchlets; the round, 1/2" blue-black berries are eaten by many animals; also by Indians. E. slope of mts.

Conif.

*30. CALIFORNIA BLACK OAK, Quercus kelloggii; Fagaceae, Fam. 30-110' high, deciduous tree, with smooth bark; leaves are bright green, 4-10" long; acorn reddish-brown; usually fine hairy, & edible after ground meal leached in warm water. Up to 8000' alt.

Conif.

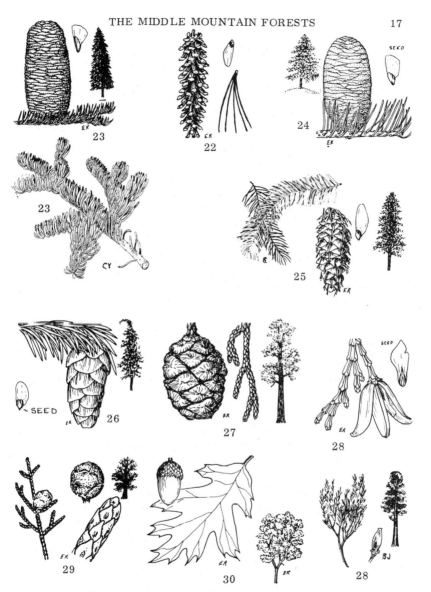

SHRUBS (sometimes become small trees)

*31. SIERRA GOOSEBERRY, <u>Ribes</u> <u>roezlii</u>; Saxifragaceae, Saxifrage Fam. A 3' high shrub, with spreading branches covered with sharp spines about 1/3" long and brown; no bristles; leaves 3/4" wide, covered with short hair below; flowers with 5 petals, purplish color, covered with hair; berry with glandular spines. Indians mixed berries with other foods for flavoring.

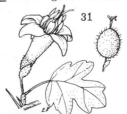

Conif.

Conif.
Str. Wd.
Sub-alp.
*32. SIERRA NEVADA CURRANT, Ribes nevadense. 3-7' high shrub, with slender, loose branches; old bark forms flakes that drop off; thin, bright green leaves; short, dense racemes (#16) with rose-colored flowers; a smooth, blue-black berry, which is edible.

Conif.
Brush
Str. Wd.
*33. THIMBLEBERRY, Rubus parviflorus; Rosaceae, Rose Fam. 3-10' high shrub with smooth branches; large, palmate (#29) and cord-ate (heart-shaped) leaves; a few large, white flowers, which turn into sweet, pale red and edible berries.

Conif.
34. MOUNTAIN MISERY, Chamaebatia foliolosa. 1-3 1/2' high, shrub, erect, with many leafy branches; bark smooth, dark-brown; 3/4-4" long leaves feel sticky; white flowers in cymes (#15); bush smells like creosote and sometimes used for medicine for colds, etc.

Conif.
Rocks
Brush
35. SIERRA CHINQUAPIN, Castanopsis sempervirens; Fagaceae, Oak and Beech Fam. 3-8' high, spreading bush with a round top, and smooth, brown bark; 1 1/2-3"long leaves are golden or reddish-brown fuzzy below, and light, grayish-yellow-green above; tiny flowers in dense spikes (#14), turning into spiny burrs. Dry places.

Conif.
Brush
*36. MARIPOSA MANZANITA, Arctostaphylos mariposa; Erica-ceae, Heath Fam. 5-15' high, erect shrub, with a reddish-brown, smooth bark; branchlets covered with tiny hairs; leaves very pale gray-green; pale pinkish or white, urn-shaped (#9) flowers; cherry-like fruit is brown and surrounded by dry, triangular bracts; has acid taste, but sometimes used by Indians to mix with other foods.

Conif
Brush
*37. GREEN-LEAVED MANZANITA, Arctostaphylos patula. 3-6 1/2' high shrub, with very crooked, stiff branches; bark smooth and bright red-brown; leaves very bright yellowish-green; pinkish flowers in large panicles (#17); fruit reddish-brown and acid; eaten by Indians.

Conif.
Brush
38. DEER BRUSH, Ceanothus integerrimus; Rhamnaceae, Buck-thorn Fam. 3-13' high shrub with diffuse branches, covered with pale green bark; the bright green leaves usually entire (#33) and smooth; end branches not spine-like; sweet-smelling flowers.

Conif.
Brush
39. MOUNTAIN WHITETHORN or SNOW BUSH, Ceanothus cor-dulatus; Rhamnaceae, Buckthorn Fam. 3-6' high shrub, with very thick branch system; branchlets rigid and thorn-like; smooth, white bark; leaves evergreen and leathery, dull greenish above, gray-green below; sweet-smelling, spicy, white flowers.

Conif.
Sage
Brush
Sub-alp.
40. HIGH SIERRA SAGEBRUSH, Artemisia rothrockii; Composi-tae, Sunflower Fam. 1/2-3' high, erect shrub, with the stems whitened with a dense fuzz and leaves usually grayish-white from the fuzz, but sometimes greenish; the tiny flower heads (#11) have 7-12 yellowish or purplish flowers (no ray flowers). Foliage with pungent odor.

HERBS

*41. MOUNTAIN STRAW-BERRY, <u>Fragaria californica</u>; Rosaceae, Rose Fam. 4-10" tall, with thin, light green leaves and usually 2 white flowers; berries bright red and edible.

Conif. Brush

42. SCARLET GILIA, <u>Ipomopsis aggregata</u>; Polemoniaceae, Phlox Fam. 4-20" high with very thin and pinnate leaves; flowers scarlet, tubular and funnel-form (#4) in a close panicle (#17); flowers may also be pink or yellow and often spotted with white or yellow. Tulare N.

Conif. Rocks Mead.

AA. SNOW PLANT, <u>Sarcodes sanguinea</u>; Monotropaceae, Indian-pipe Fam. Entire plant red, thick, fleshy, 1' tall. Feeds on humus.

Conif.

43. NORTHWEST CRIMSON COLUMBINE, Aquilegia formosa.
10-20" high herb with nodding, bright red flowers; basal leaves thin and in double sets of three leaflets; higher leaves much smaller and very scattered. Generally in moist woods; several varieties.

Sub-alp.
Conif.
Mead.

44. SHOWY PENSTEMON, Penstemon speciosus; Scrophularia-ceae, Figwort Fam. 8-32" high herb, with thick, and often spoon-shaped leaves; very showy, bright, purple-blue flowers, sympetalous, (#10) and irregular, in clusters. Usually E. side of mountains.

Conif.
Sage
Mead.

45. LITTLE ELEPHANT HEAD, Pedicularis attolens. 1-1 1/2' high herb, with 3-5" long basal and pinnately-divided (#37) leaves; the white and purple flowers look like tiny elephant heads, each with trunk. From San Bernardino Mts. north. ELEPHANT HEAD (P. groenlandica). Similar to above, but flowers larger and rose-purple.

Conif.
Mead.

46. SIERRA MULE EARS, Wyethia mollis; Compositæ, Sunflower Fam. 1 1/2-3' high herb with large, basal, ear-like leaves and small-er leaves on stem, all covered with woolly-white hair; ray flowers (#11) yellow and quite large. From Mariposa Co. N. COMMON MULE EARS (Wyethia angustifolia) has woolly-green leaves.

Conif.
Mead.
Rocks

47. LODGEPOLE PINE SENECIO, Senecio lugens. 1/2-3' herb, with a naked or few-leaved stem rising from densely-clustered, rope-like roots; yellow flowers in heads (#11), surrounded by black-tipped bracts, the heads forming cymes (#15); 10-12 conspicuous yellow ray flowers. Wet ground, from Tulare Co. N.

Conif.
Mead.

Other Common Plants Found in the Middle Mountain Forests

Water Fern, 9	Sedges, 27	Nude Buckwheat, 28
Lady Fern, 9	Long-styled Rush, 27	Red Larkspur, 28
Five-finger Fern, 9	Red Fescue Grass, 27	Giant Hyssop, 30
Rock Fern, 37	Malpais Blue Grass, 27	Hoary Buckwheat, 24
Cliff Brake, 37	Calif. Stipa Grass, 26	Sierra Stone Crop, 24
Fox-tail Pine, 22	Tickle Grass, 27	Fireweed, 30
Limber Pine, 22	Idaho Bent Grass, 27	Western Dog Violet, 30
White-bark Pine, 22		Torrey's Lupine, 29
	Mariposa Lily, 28	Pussy Paws, 28
Quaking Aspen, 10	Corn Lily, 28	Sierra Shooting Star, 30

Willows, 10
Maples, 10
Mountain Dogwood, 10
Western Azalea, 10
Box Elder, 10

Golden Brodiaea, 28
Harvest Brodiaea, 28

Squaw Currant, 23
Cinquefoils, 23, 29
Prickly Currant, 23

Indian Paint Brush, 30
Monkey Flower, 30

Bigelow Sneezeweed, 30
Bristly Aster, 31
Common Sagebrush, 38

Common Animals of the Middle Mountain Forests

Little Brown Bat, 42
California Myotis, 42
Long-eared Myotis, 42
Hairy-winged Myotis, 44
Big Brown Bat, 44
Silvery-haired Bat, 44
Red Bat, 44
Hoary Bat, 44

Black Bear, 45
Raccoon, 45
Pine Marten, 45
Fisher, 45
Short-tailed Weasel, 46
Long-tailed Weasel, 46
Mink, 46
Wolverine, 46
Striped Skunk, 46
Spotted Skunk, 46
Red Fox, 46
Coyote 46
Wildcat, 47
Mountain Lion, 47

Golden-mantled Ground
 Squirrel, 48
Lodgepole Chipmunk, 48
Sonoma Chipmunk, 48
Long-eared Chipmunk, 48
Townsend's Chipmunk, 49
Chickaree, 50
Calif. Gray Squirrel, 50
Flying Squirrel, 50

White-footed Mouse, 50
Brush Mouse, 51
Pinyon Mouse, 50
W. Harvest Mouse, 52
Dusky-footed Woodrat,
 52
Bushy-tailed Woodrat, 52
Mt. Meadow Mouse, 52
W. Red-backed Mouse, 52
Yellow-haired Porcupine,
 54

Snowshoe Hare, 54

Mule Deer, 55
Elk, 55

Birds
Turkey Vulture, 59
Goshawk, 59
Cooper's Hawk, 59
Sharp-shinned Hawk, 59

Red-tailed Hawk, 60
Golden Eagle, 60
Sparrow Hawk, 60

Sooty Grouse, 60
Mountain Quail, 60
Band-tailed Pigeon, 62

Horned Owl, 63
Flammulated Owl, 63
Pygmy Owl, 63
Spotted Owl, 63
Great Gray Owl, 63

Calliope Hummingbird,
 64
Broad-tailed Humming-
 bird, 64
Common Nighthawk, 64
Red-shafted Flicker, 65
Pileolated Woodpecker, 65
Acorn Woodpecker, 65
Lewis's Woodpecker, 65
Hairy Woodpecker, 66
White-headed Woodpeck-
 er, 66
Williamson's Sapsucker,
 66
Red-breasted Sap-
 sucker, 66

Western Flycatcher, 67
Wright's Flycatcher, 67
W. Wood Pewee, 67
Olive-sided Flycatcher,
 67
Hammond's Flycatcher,
 67

Tree Swallow, 67
Violet-green Swallow, 68
Purple Martin, 68
Steller's Jay, 68
Crow, 68
Clark's Nutcracker, 68

Chestnut-backed Chicka-
 dee, 69
Mountain Chickadee, 69
White-breasted Nut-
 hatch, 70
Red-breasted Nuthatch, 70
Pygmy Nuthatch, 70
Creeper, 70
House Wren, 70
Winter Wren, 70
Robin, 71

Hermit Thrush, 72
Varied Thrush, 71
Western Bluebird, 72
Mountain Bluebird, 72
Townsend's Solitaire, 72
Golden-crowned Kinglet, 72
Ruby-crowned Kinglet, 73

Solitary Vireo, 73
Orange-crowned Warbler,
 74
Calaveras Warbler, 74
Macgillivray's Warbler, 75
Black-throated Gray
 Warbler, 74
Audubon's Warbler, 74
Hermit Warbler, 74
Brewer's Blackbird, 75
Western Tanager, 76

Black-headed Grosbeak, 76
Evening Grosbeak, 77
Calif. Purple Finch, 76
Cassin's Finch, 76
Red Crossbill, 76
Pine Grosbeak, 76
Lesser Goldfinch, 77
Pine Siskin, 77
Chipping Sparrow, 78
Oregon Junco, 79

Reptiles
Sagebrush Lizard, 80
Western Skink, 80
Gilbert's Skink, 81
Foothill Aligator Lizard, 81
Northern Aligator Lizard, 81
Rubber Boa, 82
Mountain King Snake, 82
Racer, 82
W. Ring-neck Snake, 82

Amphibians
Rough-skinned Newt, 85
California Newt, 85
Long-toed Salamander, 85
Pacific Giant Salamander,
 86
Eschscholtz's Salamander,
 86
Slender Salamander, 86

Western Toad, 87
Pacific Tree Frog, 87

Hudsonian & Arctic-alpine Zones in mts.; courtesy So. Pac. Co.

This is the highest forest in the region, going to the edge of timberline where all trees are stunted and misshapen by the wind, It is a cold, harsh region, with very few frost-free days, and much snow. The meadows of this region are so intimately associated with the rather scattered trees of this forest that they are here considered part of it. Most of the grasses and the flowers described in the alpine meadow section (page 33) are also found here.

TREES

46. WHITE-BARK PINE, Pinus albicaulis; Pinaceae, Pine Fam.
Sub-alp. 15-50' high, evergreen; usually stunted and low with a crooked or
Conif. even lying-down trunk; the branches short and thick; the thin bark is divided into whitish-brown scales; the dark green needles are in 5's, stout and stiff, 1 1/2-3" long; purplish cones 1 1/2-3" long.

47. LIMBER PINE, Pinus flexilis. 45-80' high, evergreen, with a short, stout trunk, covered with thin and light gray to silvery bark;
Sub-alp. the old bark breaks into dark brown plates; the dark green needles are
Conif. in 5's, marked with little pits; cones light brownish-purple, 3-10" long. In Warner Mts. and E. slope Sierra from El Dorado Co. south.

48. FOXTAIL PINE, Pinus balfouriana. 20-48' high, evergreen, with stout, short branches; the branchlets are brush-like with thick
Sub-alp. clusters of the dark, blue-green needles (in 5's), which are often
Conif. whitish on the insides; cones dark red-brown, 1 1/2-3" long, covered with incurved prickles. Inner N. Coast Ranges and southern Sierras.

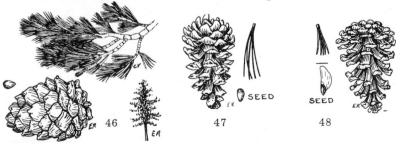

46   47   SEED   SEED   48

SHRUBS

49. ALPINE WILLOW, <u>Salix angulorum</u>; Salicaceae, Willow Fam. The <u>stems creep over the ground, usually rising only about 4"</u>; brownish or yellowish in color; leaves deep green above, paler beneath. Found from Inyo and Tulare Cos. north.

Sub-alp.
Alpine
Mead.

*50. WHITE SQUAW CURRANT, <u>Ribes cereum</u>; Saxifragaceae, Saxifrage and Gooseberry Fam. 1 1/2-3 1/2' high shrub with many branches, the branchlets covered with tiny hairs; <u>the white or pink tubular flowers in short, hanging racemes</u> (#16); berries bright red, edible. Indians made a jelly from the berries.

Sub-alp.
Conif.
Rocks
Brush

*51. ALPINE PRICKLY CURRANT, <u>Ribes montigenum</u>. 1-2' high, scraggly bush, with the stems usually bristly; leaves and most of the <u>plant covered with dense, and short hairs, often sticky to touch</u>; racemes (#16) 3-7 flowered; flowers reddish-brown or purplish; berries red, covered with glandular bristles; somewhat edible.

Sub-alp.
Rocks
Conif.

52. SHRUBBY CINQUEFOIL, <u>Potentilla fruticosa</u>; Rosaceae, Rose Fam. 1/2-4' high undershrub with many branches and very leafy stems; the brown bark shreds off; leaflets hairy-silky, flowers yellow.

Sub-alp.
Mead.
Conif.
Alpine

53. WESTERN MOUNTAIN HEATHER, <u>Cassiope mertensiana</u>; Ericaceae, Heath Fam. 4-12" high; a low and creeping bush, with evergreen leaves keeled or grooved on the back and scale-like; solitary flowers white to pinkish; many tiny, winged seeds. From Fresno and Trinity Counties north.

Sub-alp.
Rocks
Alpine

54. PURPLE MOUNTAIN HEATHER, <u>Phyllodoce breweri</u>. 4-16" high, rigid and erect shrub with linear leaves (#31); the campanulate (#3) flowers are deep rose purple or pinkish.

Sub-alp.
Alpine
Rocks

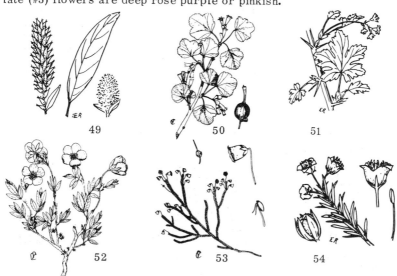

49   50   51

52   53   54

HERBS

55. HOARY BUCKWHEAT, Eriogonum marifolium; Polygonaceae,
Sub-alp. Buckwheat Fam. 1-4" high herb, covered with a dense white or hoary
Rocks (marked with black) wool; the pale, lemon-yellow flowers appear in a
Conif. tiny umbel (#12), almost like a head (#11), surrounded by leaf-like
bracts. Found mainly from Fresno Co. north.

BB. SNAKEWEED, Polygonum bistortoides; Polygonaceae, Poly-
Sub-alp. gonum Fam. 8-25" high; several erect, hairless, slender and simple
Str.Wd. stems rise from a thick, level rootstock; spikes pink or white.
Conif.

CC₊ SULPHUR FLOWER, Eriogonum umbellatum. 3-6" high.
Sub-alp. Few to many branches from woody base; leaves white hairy beneath;
Sage bright, sulphur-yellow flowers in ball-like clusters. Dry slopes.
Conif.

56. COVILLE'S COLUMBINE, Aquilegia pubescens; Ranuncula-
Sub-alp. ceae, Buttercup Fam. 9-12" herb with solitary, showy, usually yel-
Rocks low flowers, standing erect instead of nodding (as in most columbines);
Alpine stem leaves few, 3-pinnate, covered, at least above, with tiny hairs.
Found from Tuolumne Co. to Tulare and Inyo Cos.

57. SIERRA STONE-CROP, Sedum obtusatum; Crassulaceae,
Sub-alp. Stonecrop Fam. 2-6' stems, rising from a thick, horizontal root-
Conif. stock; basal leaves (#27) spoon-like, thick and fleshy and pale green;
Rocks the yellow or cream-colored petals of the flowers (#2) are only united
Alpine near their bases. Tulare to Plumas Co.; also Trinity Co. north.

58. SIERRA PENSTEMON, Penstemon heterodoxus; Scrophulari-
Sub-alp. aceae, Figwort Fam. 3-10" herb with slender stems; thin, dark
Alpine green leaves, and with the dark bluish-purple of the flowers tipped
Rocks
Mead. with brownish-yellow beards. From Tulare Co. to Plumas Co.

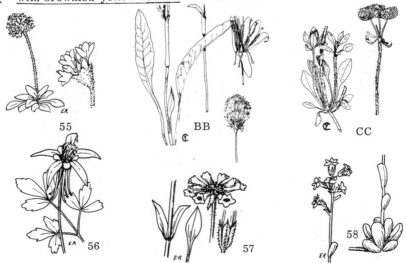

55   BB   ℂ   ℂ   CC

56   57   58

Common Plants of the Sub-alpine Forest and Meadows

Lady Fern, 9
Common Brake Fern, 15
Western White Pine, 16
Lodgepole Pine, 15
Mountain Hemlock, 16
Douglas Phlox, 37

Corn Lily, 28
Brewer's Cinquefoil, 28
Pussy Paws, 28
Sierra Nevada Currant, 18
Small Tiger Lily, 9

Crimson Columbine, 20
Indian Paint Brush, 30
Monkey Flower, 30
Sierra Bristly Aster, 31
High Sierra Sagebrush, 18

Common Animals of the Sub-alpine Forest and Meadows

Vagrant Shrew, 42
Mount Lyell Shrew, 42
Adorned Shrew, 42
Shrew-mole, 42
Little Brown Bat, 42
Black Bear, 45
Pine Marten, 45
Short-tailed Weasel, 46
Long-tailed Weasel, 46
Badger, 46
Wolverine, 46
Red Fox, 46
Coyote, 46
Mountain Lion, 47
Marmot, 48
Golden-mantled Ground Squirrel, 48
Belding Ground Squirrel, 48
Lodgepole Chipmunk, 48
Alpine Chipmunk, 48
Chickaree, 50
Mt. Pocket Gopher, 50
White-footed Mouse, 50
Bushy-tailed Woodrat, 52
Mountain Meadow Mouse, 52
Long-tailed Meadow Mouse, 52
Mt. Lemming Mouse, 52
Pacific Jumping Mouse, 52
Mountain Beaver, 54
Yellow-haired Porcupine, 54
Pika, 54

White-tailed Hare, 54
Snowshoe Hare, 54
Mule Deer, 55
Mountain Sheep, 55

Birds

Turkey Vulture, 59
Goshawk, 59
Cooper's Hawk, 59
Red-tailed Hawk, 59
Golden Eagle, 60
Sparrow Hawk, 60
Sooty Grouse, 60
Horned Owl, 63
Saw-whet Owl, 63
Great Gray Owl, 63
Common Nighthawk, 64
Calliope Hummingbird, 64
Red-shafted Flicker, 65
Pileolated Woodpecker, 65
Hairy Woodpecker, 66
White-headed Woodpecker, 66
Black-headed Three-toed Woodpecker, 66
Williamson's Sapsucker, 66
Red-breasted Sapsucker, 66
Hammond's Flycatcher, 67
Wright's Flycatcher, 67
Western Wood Pewee, 67
Olive-sided Flycatcher, 67
Horned Lark, 68

Steller's Jay, 68
Raven, 68
Clark's Nutcracker, 68
Mountain Chickadee, 69
White-breasted Nuthatch, 70
Red-breasted Nuthatch, 70
Brown Creeper, 70
House Wren, 70
Winter Wren, 70
Robin, 71
Hermit Thrush, 72
Western Blue Bird, 72
Mountain Blue Bird, 72
Townsend's Solitaire, 72
Golden-crowned Kinglet, 72
Ruby-crowned Kinglet, 73
Pipit, 73
Warbling Vireo, 73
Orange-crowned Warbler, 74
Audubon's Warbler, 74
Hermit Warbler, 74
Macgillivray's Warbler, 75
Wilson's Warbler, 75
Western Tanager, 76
Evening Grosbeak, 76
Cassin's Purple Finch, 76
Red Crossbill, 76
Pine Grosbeak, 76
Pine Siskin, 77
Chipping Sparrow, 78
Oregon Junco, 78

Reptiles

Sagebrush Lizard, 80
Western Rattlesnake, 84

Amphibians

Mt. Lyell Salamander, 86
Pacific Tree Toad, 87

MIDDLE MOUNTAIN MEADOWS

Photo by U.S. Forest Service.

These are the meadows found associated with the middle mountain forests already described. They lie deep under the snow in the winter, but, with the coming of the warm spring and summer days, they often turn into veritable paradises of wild flowers, attracting birds and other animals to their lush greenness. When overgrazed, however, by cattle or sheep, they become very poor-looking, gullied by destructive erosion and a lesson in the need for intelligent conserving of our natural resources.

GRASSES

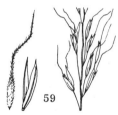

59. CALIFORNIA STIPA GRASS, Stipa californica; Gramineae, Grass Fam. 2-5' high grass, with plume-like tips to the florets or small grass-flowers (see illustration this page), the plumes or awns bent in two places; the sheaths that protect the florets are smooth and the leaf-blades are flat and rather scattered.

Mead.
Conif.

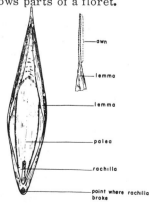

PARTS OF TYPICAL GRASS

To help you identify grasses, the picture to the left helps you to identify parts of a complete grass. The picture below shows parts of a floret.

spikelet
awn
rachis
glume
pedicle
floret
blade
midrib
collar
sheath
ligule
node
internode
culm or stem
PANICLE
roots start at node
root

awn
lemma
lemma
palea
rachilla
point where rachilla broke

60. ROUGH-HAIR GRASS or TICKLE GRASS, Agrostis scabra. 8-32" tall grass, with delicate slender stems and a very diffuse panicle (#17), sometimes 1' long.

Mead.
Conif.

61. IDAHO BENT GRASS, Agrostis idahoensis. 4-12" high grass, with slender stems; a loosely-spreading panicle (#17), though not as much as in the above grass, and shorter branches.

Mead.
Conif.

62. MALPAIS BLUE GRASS, Poa scabrella. 1 1/2-3 1/2' tall grass with rough-feeling stems and sheaths of the florets; leaf blades mainly basal (#27); a narrow panicle (#17), though it may be wider at its base. There are many kinds of bluegrasses in the Sierras. To 5000'.

Mead.
Conif.
Str. Wd.

63. RED FESCUE GRASS, Festuca rubra. 1 1/4-3 1/4" high grass with the lower leaf sheaths often purple and always smooth; the leaf blades feel smooth and soft and are usually folded or rolled inwards; the pale green spikelets are often tinged with purple. Up to 8500'.

Mead.
Conif.
Str. Wd.

64. SEDGES, Carex species; Cyperaceae, Sedge Fam. Very numerous species, all characterized by triangular-shaped stems, and long, narrow leaves in 3 ranks; the stems form one to many spikes. Very common in damp meadows at all altitudes.

Mead.
Conif.
Sub-alp.
Str. Wd.
Water

65. LONG-STYLED RUSH, Juncus longistylus; Juncaceae, Rush Fam. 8-16" high, with erect, loosely-tufted stems, circular in cross-section; the flat, grass-like, basal leaves have rough sheaths over the stem; florets greenish-brown with transparent margins. There are many kinds of rushes in the mountains, all similar to this rush.

Mead.
Conif.
Sub-alp.

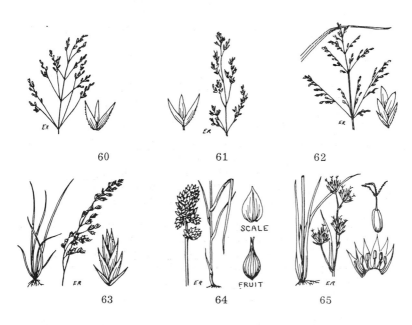

60   61   62

63   64   65

HERBS

Mead.
Sub-alp.   67. CORN LILYor FALSE HELLEBORE, Veratrum californicum;
Str.Wd. Melanthaceae, Bunch Flower Fam. 1-3 1/4' tall, with stout stems;
Conif. very large, parallel-veined leaves (#35); the white flowers have green-
ish veins and are in panicles (#17). Up to 10, 000'.

Mead.   *68. GOLDEN BRODIAEA, Brodiaea lutea; Liliaceae, Lily Fam.
Conif. 8-16" high herb, with a few linear (#31) and basal (#27) leaves; large
Brush yellow flowers marked with brown midveins, in an open umbel (#12);
Anthers of stamens oval and creamy-white to blue. From Butte Co. S.

            *69. HARVEST BRODIAEA, Brodiaea coronaria. 8-24" high herb
         with narrow leaves about as long as stem; flowers violet-purple and
Mead.   funnel-form (#4); umbels (#12) with 2-11 flowers.   Like other bro-
Conif.   diaeas it rises from an edible white bulb sheathed in a brown, fibrous
cover. Mainly found in the lower meadows of Ponderosa Pine Forest.

            70. MARIPOSA LILY, Calochortus venustus.   4-32" high, with
Mead.   very stiff and erect stem; umbels (#12) of 1-4 white or lilac flowers,
Conif.   each petal with a dark eye-spot in the middle and a reddish mark near
the top; 1-2 basal leaves. Lower meadows from Tulare Co. north.

            71. CALIFORNIA BLUE-EYED GRASS, Sisyrinchium bellum;
Mead.   Iridaceae, Iris Fam. 4-20" high herb, with leaves as long as stem
Str. Wd. from base, plus smaller leaves born on stem; flowers violet-purple
in color, each petal tipped with a point. In lower meadows.

            72. NUDE BUCKWHEAT, Eriogonum latifolium; Polygonaceae,
Mead.   Buckwheat Fam.   8-40" high, but the high Sierra form is around 8-
Conif.   10" high; a perennial with spreading, basal (#27) leaves, covered
Rocks with white fuzz below; white flowers in heads with the sepals (#1a)
Brush having rose-colored veins. Usually on dry or rocky slopes.

            73. PUSSY-PAWS, Calyptridium umbellatum; Portulacaceae, the
Mead.   Purslane Fam. Very low, 2-4" high herb, with spreading stems;
Conif.   leaves spoon-shaped, usually basal, sometimes some small leaves
Sub-alp. on stems; the pink or white flowers form round balls. Sandy soil.

            74. RED LARKSPUR, Delphinium nudicaule; Ranunculaceae, But-
Mead.   tercup Fam. 1-2' high herb, with slender, usually naked stems;
Conif.   basal leaves somewhat thick; a loose raceme (#16) of yellow flowers,
Brush tipped with red, and the sepals (#1a) red; seeds winged; flowers shaped
like a cornucopia. Found mainly from Mariposa Co. north.

            75. MONKSHOOD, Aconitum columbianum. Stem 2-4' tall; all
Mead.   leaves palmately-lobed or divided, 3-5 times; flowers purplish-blue
Conif.   in a loosely few flowered raceme; the uppermost sepal in the form of
a hood, enclosing the upper 2-hooded petals; fruit of 2-6 follicles or
pods. Found in moist areas, especially near willows.

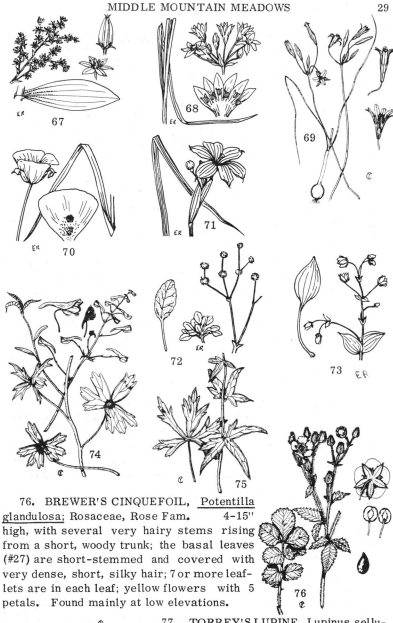

76. BREWER'S CINQUEFOIL, Potentilla glandulosa; Rosaceae, Rose Fam. 4-15" high, with several very hairy stems rising from a short, woody trunk; the basal leaves (#27) are short-stemmed and covered with very dense, short, silky hair; 7 or more leaflets are in each leaf; yellow flowers with 5 petals. Found mainly at low elevations.

Mead.
Conif.
Sub-alp.
Brush
Rocks

77. TORREY'S LUPINE, Lupinus sellulus; Fabaceae, Pea Fam. 5-8" high herb, with crowded basal leaves and no woody base; 6-8 leaflets covered with flattened, and silky hairs; flowers violet blue, with the center of the top petal (or banner) touched with yellow or purple. From Tulare Co. north.

Mead.
Conif.
Sage

Mead.
Conif.
Str. Wd.
Sub-alp.
78. WESTERN DOG VIOLET, Viola adunca; Violaceae, Violet Fam. 2-2 1/2" herb, rising from a narrow, branching rootstock; basal leaves with low, broad teeth; the violet-blue petals have tufts of slender hairs at bases and are 1/2" or more long.

Mead.
Brush
Conif.
79. FIREWEED, Epilobium angustifolium; Onagraceae, Evening Primrose Fam. 2-8' high herb with 1 or few slender, erect stems; leaves linear-lanceolate (#30-31), with the side-veins forming loops along the edges of the leaves; racemes (#16) with many large lilac, white, rose or purple flowers. Mainly in burned areas.

Mead.
Alpine
Sub-alp.
Conif.
80. SIERRA SHOOTING STAR, Dodecatheon jeffreyi; Primulaceae, Primrose Fam. 14-24" high herb, with 6-16" long leaves, and distinctive reversed flowers with reddish-purple anthers (#1d), dark purple band at throat and rose-pink to yellowish petals. ALPINE SHOOTING STAR, D. alpinum. Similar, but smaller, shorter leaves.

Mead.
Conif.
Str. Wd.
81. GIANT HYSSOP or NETTLE-LEAVED HORSE-MINT, Agastache urticifolia; Labiatae, Mint Fam. 3-6' herb, with several erect stems, ending in distinctive spikes (#14) of light, violet-purple flowers; leaves shining, sometimes irritating to skin; square stems.

Mead.
Sub-alp.
Alpine
Str. Wd.
82. CULBERTSON'S INDIAN PAINT-BRUSH, Castilleja culbertsonii. 4-8" high herb, covered with tiny hairs; somewhat sticky or glandular on lower parts; numerous stems; the bracts surrounding the flowers are purple; the flowers dark green with thin purple margins. From Tulare Co. to Fresno Co.

Mead.
Conif.
83. GREAT RED INDIAN PAINT BRUSH, Castilleja miniata. 16-32" high herb, smooth or hairy; the stems form clusters; the bracts surrounding the flowers are usually bright red or vermilion, but sometimes duller red; petals dark green with thin red margins, usually 3/4-1 1/4" long; flowers (as in most paint brushes) in spike-like racemes (#16). Many varieties of paint brushes in our mountains.

Mead.
Str. Wd.
Conif.
84. PRIMROSE MONKEY FLOWER, Mimulus primuloides. This is just one among many kinds of monkey flowers in the mts. Up to 2" high, usually with a few flower stems rising from a basal cluster of leaves; flower 1/2-3/4" long, yellow, one petal deeply yellow and very hairy, spotted with brown or with one large brown spot.

Mead.
Conif.
Sub-alp.
85. BIGELOW SNEEZEWEED, Helenium bigelovii; Compositae, Sunflower Fam. 2-4' high herb, branching, with 4-10" long leaves, sometimes with very tiny hairs, often resin-like dotted; the yellow ray flowers (#11) droop down from the brown or brownish-yellow ball of disk flowers. May cause sneezing when pollen is breathed.

Mead.
86. WHITE YARROW, Achillea millefolium. 1 1/2-3 1/4' high perennial herb, with a simple stem and large leaves divided into numerous fine segments; head (11) in corymbs (#13) at end of stem; each head with a few white ray flowers (#11) and many yellow disk flowers.

CAPSULE

SINGLE FLOWER

78 79 80 81 82 83 84 85 86

87. SIERRA BRISTLY ASTER, Haplo-pappus apargioides. 3-11" high herb, with several stems rising from a very thick root, which is sheathed in old leaves; leaves mainly in a basal tuft, 1 1/2-4 1/2" long; heads (#11) 1-3, surrounded by pur-plish-tipped bracts; both ray and disk flow-ers yellow; seeds surrounded by dirty-yel-low bristles. San Bernardino-Plumas Co.

HEAD

87

DISK FLOWER

Mead.
Rocks
Conif.
Sub-alp.
Alpine

88

88. CALIFORNIA CONE FLOWER, Rud-beckia californica. 2-6' tall herb, with a simple stem topped by a solitary head (#11) with showy, yellow ray flowers & dark brown or purplish disk flowers. BLACK-EYED SUSAN, R. hirta. Similar, with rough, hairy and branching stems.

Mead.

Common Animals of the Middle Mountain Meadows

Broad-footed Mole, 41
Shrew-mole, 42
Vagrant Shrew, 42
Adorned Shrew, 42
Yosemite Shrew, 42
Dusky Shrew, 42

Little Brown Bat, 42
California Myotis, 42
Long-eared Myotis, 42
Small-footed Myotis, 44
Big Brown Bat, 44
Red Bat, 44
Hoary Bat, 44
Silvery-haired Bat, 44

Black Bear, 45
Pine Marten, 45
Short-tailed Weasel, 46
Long-tailed Weasel, 46
Mink 46
Badger, 46
Wolverine, 46
Striped Skunk, 46
Spotted Skunk, 46
Red Fox, 46
Coyote, 46
Wildcat, 47
Mountain Lion, 47
Marmot, 48
California Ground
    Squirrel, 48
Golden-mantled Ground
    Squirrel, 48
Belding Ground Squirrel,
    48
Mt. Pocket Gopher, 50
Botta Pocket Gopher, 50

White-footed Mouse, 50
W. Harvest Mouse, 52
Bushy-tailed Woodrat,
    52

Mt. Meadow Mouse, 52
Oregon Meadow Mouse,
    52
Long-tailed Meadow
    Mouse, 52
Jumping Mouse, 52

Pika, 54
Black-tailed Hare, 54
White-tailed Hare, 54

Mule Deer, 55
Elk, 55

Birds
Great Blue Heron, 57
Canada Goose, 57

Goshawk, 59
Sharp-shinned Hawk, 59
Golden Eagle, 60
Swainson's Hawk, 60
Red-tailed Hawk, 60
Marsh Hawk, 60
Sparrow Hawk, 60

Mountain Quail, 60
Mourning Dove, 60
Killdeer, 62
Horned Owl, 63

Common Nighthawk, 64
Rufous Hummingbird, 64
Calliope Hummingbird,
    64
Allen's Hummingbird, 64
Broad-tailed Humming-
    bird, 64

Red-shafted Flicker, 65
Black Swift, 64

Tree Swallow, 67
Purple Martin, 68
Violet-green Swallow, 68

Crow, 68
Black-billed Magpie, 68
Bush-tit, 69
Robin, 71
Western Bluebird, 72
Mountain Bluebird, 72

Pipit, 73

Brewer's Blackbird, 75
Bullock's Oriole, 75

Black-headed Grosbeak, 76
Pine Siskin, 77
Lesser Goldfinch, 77

Vesper Sparrow, 78
Chipping Sparrow, 78
White-crowned Sparrow, 78
Lincoln's Sparrow, 78
Oregon Junco, 79

Reptiles
Western Fence Lizard, 80
Sagebrush Lizard, 80
Western Skink, 80
Gilbert's Skink, 81

Mountain King Snake, 82
Common King Snake, 82
Racer, 82
Western Gopher Snake, 84
Pacific Rattlesnake, 84

Amphibians
Spade-foot Toad, 87
Western Toad, 87
Yosemite Toad, 87
Pacific Tree Frog, 87
Yellow-legged Frog, 87
Red-legged Frog, 88
Leopard Frog, 88

Long-toed Salamander, 85

ALPINE FELL FIELDS OR MEADOWS

Photo courtesy of Sierra Club.

This is a land of ice, snow and rocks above tree growth, a land where there is a brief and almost violent growth of wild flowers in mid-summer, and where only a few animals can find food to support themselves. The growing season lasts only a month to 7 weeks. The sun is very bright in summer on the snow, but the temperature rarely goes above 60 degrees.

Because of limitations in space the common alpine plants are pictured here with only brief descriptions. Most of the plants described here are also found, though usually less commonly, in the sub-alpine meadows. Thus, no habitats are listed here on the margins.

89. HELLER'S SEDGE, Carex helleri; Cyperaceae, Sedge Fam. 2-12" high, in dense tufts. From Tulare Co. north.

90. BREWER'S SEDGE, Carex breweri. 4-11" high; leaf blades narrow and rough; a solitary spike (#14). From Mt. Whitney north.

91. SMALL SHEEP FESCUE, Festuca brachyphylla; Gramineae, Grass Fam. 3-6" high, in dense tuft; flower spikes rough to touch.

89

90

91

92. TIMBERLINE BLUE GRASS, Poa rupicola. 4-8" high, stiff stems in tufts; Spikelets purplish-colored. From Tulare Co. north.

92

93. SUKSDORF'S BLUEGRASS, Poa suksdorfii. 4-8" high; tufted; leaf-sheaths loose, paper-like and smooth. From Ventura Co. N.

94. SPIKED WOOD RUSH, Luzula spicata; Juncaceae, Rush Fam. 4-16" high; leaves are stiffly erect; very dense groups of brown and nodding flowers; channels appear in leaves. From Tulare Co. north.

HERBS

95. OVAL-LEAVED BUCKWHEAT, Eriogonum ovalifolium; Polygonaceae, Buckwheat Fam. 3-4" high; white woolly all over;extremely numerous leaves; flowers with soft, straight hairs, petals white with red veins. From Tulare Co. north.

96. MOUNTAIN SORREL, Oxyria digyna. 2-10" high; the greenish flowers often have red sepals (#1a); in compact panicles; acid juice.

97. BREWER'S WHITLOW GRASS, Draba breweri; Cruciferae, Mustard Fam. 1-4" high, cushion-like herb, with basal, tufted, grayish leaves; white petals. From Tulare Co. north.

98. LEMMON'S DRABA, Draba lemmonii. 1-3" high; very compact leaf bunches; petals yellow; usually in rocks.

99. WHITE-MOUNTAIN DRABA, Draba oligosperma. 1 1/2-1 3/4" high; leaves leather-like and densely overlapping on stem; petals yellow. Found in central Sierra Nevada and White Mts.

100. BROAD-PODDED ROCK FLOWER, Phoenicaulis eurycarpa. 1-2" high, covered with short hairs; leaves 2/5-2/3" long, oblanceolate and hairy; few flowers with yellow petals; silvery seeds. Tulare and Inyo Cos. north to Tuolumne Co.

101. SHOCKLEY'S IVESIA, Ivesia shockleyi; Rosaceae, Rose Fam. 3/4-4" high; pallid green, delicate-looking plant, densely covered with tiny, glandular hairs; 7-10 pairs leaflets; yellow, disc-like flowers; 3 pistils. From Tulare Co. north.

102. DIVERSE-LEAVED CINQUEFOIL, Potentilla diversifolia. 4-12" high; slender stems and a few hairy leaves; petals notched.

103. ROCK FRINGE, Epilobium obcordatum; Onagraceae, Evening Primrose Fam. 2-6"; partly creeping on ground; purple or rose-colored flowers; often forms dense mats. From Tulare Co. north.

104. ALPINE SPINY RATTLEWEED, Astragalus tegetarius; Leguminosae, Pea Fam. 3-4" high; often lies on ground; leaflets rigid and spine-tipped. From Tulare Co. north.

105. SIERRA PODISTERA, Podistera nevadensis; Umbelliferae, Carrot Fam. 1-2" high; many stems from woody trunk; orange-yellow to purple flowers. From San Bernardino Mts. and north. 105

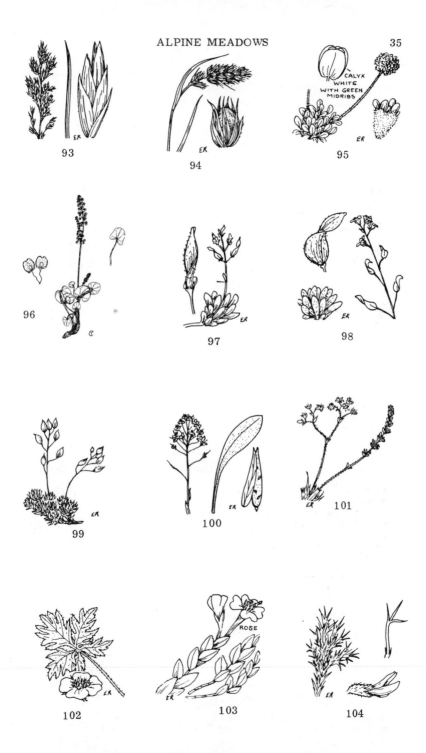

93

94

CALYX
WHITE
WITH GREEN
MIDRIBS

95

96

97

98

99

100

101

102

ROSE

103

104

106. SKY PILOT, Polemonium eximium; Polemoniaceae, Phlox
Fam. Leaves and stems glandular-sticky, with musky odor; funnel-
like flowers blue. Found from Tulare Co. to Tuolumne Co.

107. SIERRA NIEVITAS, Crypthanta nubigena; Boraginaceae,
Borage Fam. 2-6" high; hairy and bristly all over; white flowers;
plant arising from a densely leafy and branched root-crown.

108. DWARF ALPINE INDIAN PAINT BRUSH, Castilleja nana;
Scrophulariaceae, Figwort Fam. 2-10" high; irregular flowers
marked with purple, white and green; bracts yellow to purple-red.

ER   106   ER   107   108   ER

Other Common Plants Found in Alpine Meadows

Alpine Willow, 23   Sierra Penstemon, 24   *Sierra Bristly Aster, 31
Coville's Columbine, 24   Sierra Shooting Star, 30   *High Sierra Sagebrush, 18
Sierra Stonecrop, 24   Culbertson's Indian
Purple Mt. Heather, 23   Paintbrush, 30

Common Animals

Mammals   Long-tailed Meadow   Clark's Nutcracker, 68
Wolverine, 46   Mouse, 52   Robin, 71
Short-tailed Weasel, 46   Pika, 54   Mountain Bluebird, 72
Mountain Lion, 47   Mule Deer, 55   Rosy Finch, 76
Alpine Chipmunk, 48   Mountain Sheep, 55   Siskin, 77
Mountain Pocket Gopher,   Oregon Junco, 79
    50   Birds   White-crowned Sparrow, 78
White-footed Mouse, 50   Horned Lark, 68

Common Animals Found in Pinyon-Juniper Woodland on Lower East Side of Sierra.

Mammals   Big-horn Sheep, 55   Pinyon Jay, 68
White-footed Mouse, 51   Birds   Plain Titmouse, 69
White-tailed Hare, 54   Broad-tailed Humming-
Coyote, 46   bird, 64   Reptiles
                                                         Sagebrush Lizard, 80
                                                         Des. Striped Whipsnake, 82

In and Near Buildings

Brush Mouse, 51   Norway Rat, 53   House Wren, 70
House Mouse, 53   White-footed Mouse, 50   House Sparrow, 74

ROCKY AREAS AND CLIFFS
of middle altitudes

109. ROCK FERN, Cryptogramma acrostichoides. Fronds 4-12" long, both short-stalked and long-stalked. Scales rusty to dark brown or striped; the fronds form thick clusters; fertile leaves with yellow stems.

Rocks
Conif.

110. CLIFF BRAKE, Onychium densum. 6000-8000' in Sierra Nevada, 1000-6500' in Coast Ranges. Many crowded fronds, 2-12" high; underground stem with shining brown scales.

Rocks
Conif.

111. DOUGLAS PHLOX, Phlox douglassii. 1 1/2-2" high, with woody base; leaves with stiff hairs; flowers pale pink to white. Found mostly on east side of mts. from Tulare Co. to Alpine Co.

Rocks
Mead.
Sub-alp.

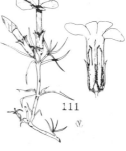

109   110   111

Other Common Plants of Rocky Areas

Five-finger Fern, 9	Sierra Chinquapin, 18	Scarlet Gilia, 19
Sword Fern, 9	Sierra Stonecrop, 24	Sierra Penstemon, 24
Brake Fern, 15	W. Mountain Heather, 23	Sierra Bristly Aster, 31
Hoary Buckwheat, 24	Purple Mt. Heather, 23	Sierra Mule Ears, 20
Coville's Columbine, 24	Torrey's Lupine, 29	Most of Alpine plants, 33

Common Animals of Rocks and Cliffs

All Myotis Bats, 42, 44	Brush Mouse, 51	Raven, 68
Big Brown Bat, 44	W. Harvest Mouse, 52	Canyon Wren, 70
Ring-tailed Cat, 45	Bushy-tailed Woodrat, 52	Rock Wren, 70
Pine Marten, 45	Pika, 54	Rosy Finch, 76
Short-tailed Weasel, 46	Mountain Sheep, 55	
Long-tailed Weasel, 46		**Reptiles**
Wolverine, 46	**Birds**	W. Fence Lizard, 80
Coyote 46	Turkey Vulture, 59	Sagebrush Lizard, 80
Mountain Lion, 47	Sparrow Hawk, 60	Western Rattlesnake, 84
Wildcat, 47	Golden Eagle, 60	
Marmot, 48	Red-tailed Hawk, 60	**Amphibians**
Calif. Ground Squirrel, 48	Horned Owl, 63	Mt. Lyell Salamander, 86
Golden-mantled Ground Squirrel, 48	Black Swift, 64	Limestone Salamander, 86
Alpine Chipmunk, 48	White-throated Swift, 64	Black Salamander, 87
White-footed Mouse, 50	Belted Kingfisher, 65	Shasta Salamander, 86
	Violet-green Swallow, 67	Canyon Tree Frog, 87

BRUSHLAND AND SAGEBRUSH AREAS

Brushland in mountains; photo courtesy U. S. Forest Service.

Burned over areas in the mountains temporarily spring up with brush, including such species as:

*Calif. Stipa Grass, 26	High Sierra Sagebrush, 18	Fireweed, 30
Manzanita, 18	Brewer's Cinquefoil, 29	Torrey's Lupine, 29
Deer Brush, 18	Nude Buckwheat, 28	Mountain Strawberry, 19
Mt. Whitethorn, 18	Red Larkspur, 28	*Showy Penstemon, 20
Sierra Chinquapin, 18	Golden Brodiaea, 28	*Sierra Mule's Ears, 20

Sage
Conif.

112. COMMON SAGEBRUSH, Artemisia tridentata; Fam. Compositae, Sunflowers. In certain areas that are very dry this very strong-smelling, silvery-gray bush occupies many acres. 2-15' high; 3-6 or even 12 flowers in a head; no ray flowers. In the mountains, Common Sagebrush is often almost the only plant in the sagebrush habitat.

(Animals and plants most commonly found in the sagebrush habitat are marked with a * in the lists below and above.)

Common Animals of Brushland and Sagebrush

Mammals
Adorned Shrew, 42
All Myotis Bats, 42-44
Big Brown Bat, 44
Black Bear, 45
Ring-tailed Cat, 45
Spotted Skunk, 46
Gray Fox, 46
Coyote, 46
Wildcat, 47
Mountain Lion, 47
Calif. Ground Squirrel, 48
*Least Chipmunk, 48
Long-eared Chipmunk, 48
Sonoma Chipmunk, 48
Merriam's Chipmunk, 49
White-footed Mouse, 50
Brush Mouse, 51
West. Harvest Mouse, 52
Dusky-footed Woodrat, 52
Black-tailed Hare, 54

White-tailed Hare, 54
Mule Deer, 55
*Mountain Sheep, 55

Birds
Turkey Vulture, 59
Golden Eagle, 60
Red-tailed Hawk, 60
California Quail, 60
Mountain Quail, 60
Horned Owl, 63
Allen's Hummingbird, 64
Wright's Flycatcher, 67
Violet Green Swallow, 67
*Black-billed Magpie, 68
Bush-tit, 69
House Wren, 70
Varied Thrush, 71
Orange-crowned Warbler, 74
Calaveras Warbler, 74
Macgillivray's Warbler, 75
Wilson's Warbler, 75

Lesser Goldfinch, 77
Lazuli Bunting, 78
Towhees, 77-78
Fox Sparrow, 78
*Vesper Sparrow, 78
White-crowned Sparrow, 78
*Sage or Bell's Sparrow, 78
*Black-throated Sparrow, 78

Reptiles
Western Fence Lizard, 80
Sagebrush Lizard, 80
Western Skink, 80
Foothill Alligator Lizard, 81
Racer, 82
*Desert Striped Whipsnake, 82
Calif. Striped Whipsnake, 82
Common King Snake, 82
Mountain King Snake, 82
Sharp-tailed Snake, 82
Pacific Rattlesnake, 84

Amphibians
Calif. Slender Salamander, 86
Canyon Tree Toad, 87

FRESH WATER AREAS

Photo courtesy U. S. Forest Service.

Fresh water areas in the Sierra Nevada include streams, lakes, ponds and swampy or boggy areas. The illustrations below give examples of some of the common fresh water plants.

113. COMMON TULE, Scirpus acutus; Cyperaceae, Sedge Fam. Up to 16' tall with stems 3/4" thick, forming dense stands in shallows.

114. CREEPING SPIKE RUSH, Heleocharis palustris. 1 1/2-4' tall, with leaves forming only basal sheaths; terminal spike to 1/2".

115. BROAD-LEAVED CATTAIL, Typha latifolia; Typhaceae, Cattail Fam. 3-8' tall; 12-16 very long, flat, light-green leaves.

116. COMMON WATER PLANTAIN, Alisma triviale; Alismataceae, Water Plantain Fam. Flowers in pyramidal, whorled panicles.

*117. BROAD-LEAVED ARROWHEAD, Sagittaria sp. Milky juice; leaves with sheaths on their bases; flowers in whorls of three. The tubers were often eaten by Indians, hence called Tule Potatoes.

118. COMMON FLOATING PONDWEED, Potamogeton natans; Potamogetonaceae, Pond Weed Fam. Most pond weeds have wide floating leaves and narrow, submerged leaves. Floating leaves are slightly heart-shaped; submerged leaves are reticulate-veined.

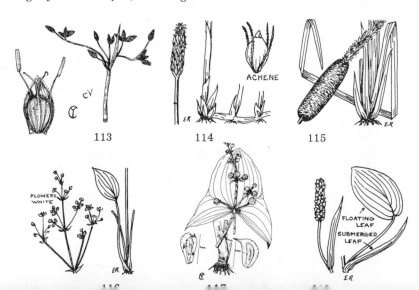

119. WATER BUTTERCUP, <u>Ranunculus aquatilus</u>; Ranunculaceae, Buttercup Fam. Submerged stems generally 8-24" long; submerged leaves thread-like; above water leaves 3-lobed or parted; the fbwers have light green sepals and 5 white petals, 10-25 stamens.

120. MARE'S TAIL, <u>Hippuris vulgaris</u>; Haloragaceae, Water-milfoil Fam. 8-24" tall, erect stems; leaves in whorls of 7-10; the very tiny flowers have no petals. Usually found below 9000'.

121. COMMON BLADDERWORT, <u>Utricularia vulgaris</u>; Lentibulariaceae. 1-3' long underwater stems; yellow flower brown-striped.

122. INDIAN POND LILY, <u>Nuphar polysepalum</u>; Nymphaeaceae, Water Lily Fam. Distinctive large flowers, usually tinged red on yellow.

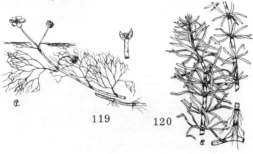

119　　120　　　　　　　　　121

122

Other Plants Found in Fresh Water

Sedges, page 27　　　　　Rushes, page 27

Common Fresh Water Animals

Mammals
Water Shrew, p. 42
Mink, 45
River Otter, 46
Beaver, 50
Nutria (may be
found in Sierra;
looks like very
large, stout,
brown rat, with
grayish muzzle
and round, al-
most hairless
tail.)

Birds
Eared Grebe, 57
Pied-billed Grebe, 57
Great Blue Heron, 57
Canada Goose, 57
Mallard, 58

Green-winged Teal, 58
Shoveller, 58
Wood Duck, 58
Bufflehead, 58
Com. Merganser, 58
Killdeer, 62
Common Snipe, 62
Spotted Sandpiper, 62
Ring-billed Gull, 62
California Gull, 62
Belted Kingfisher, 65
Dipper, 70

Reptiles
Com. Garter Snake, 84
West. Garter Snake, 84

Amphibians
Rough-skinned Newt, 85
California Newt, 85
Long-toed Salamander,
85

Pacific Giant Salamander,
86
Eschscholtz's Salamander,
86
Spade-foot Toad, 87
Western Toad, 87
Yosemite Toad, 87
Pacific Tree Toad, 87
Canyon Tree Toad, 87
Yellow-legged Frog, 88
Red-legged Frog, 88

Leopard Frog, 88

Fish (see page 89)

MAMMALS

Mammals are animals usually covered with hair or fur who give milk to their young. As many mammals are more likely to be seen in the dusk of evening or early morning, when it is hard to see them clearly, it is useful to be able to make a quick judgment as to their comparative sizes. In this book we have tried to show the pictures of animals in groups of comparative size (for example, all the carnivores are grouped together by comparative size). Besides this, and for a basis of constant comparison, we use the four common mammals pictured below as examples, marking other animals shown as "raccoon +" (meaning larger than a raccoon), "rat -" (somewhat smaller than a rat), "mouse size" (same size as a mouse), and so on. Lengths given are usually for body and head only.

House Mouse
3-4"

House Rat 8-11"

Cat   15-18"

Raccoon
2-3' long

Study the pictures that follow for body shape and color pattern, then study the descriptions and details about habits, noting particularly the habitats in which each mammal likes to live. Remember that wild mammals can best be approached by moving very slowly and quietly and wearing clothes colored like the surroundings.

A. ORDER MARSUPIALIA, Marsupials.
Prehensile tail; ♀ with pocket.

1. VIRGINIA OPOSSUM, Didel-
phis virginiana; Didelphidae,
Opossum Fam. Cat size; 15-
28" long. Color grayish; thumb of hind
foot without nail; tail scaly; coarse hair
and bad smell distinctive. Introduced.

Str. Wd.

B. Order INSECTIVORES. Numerous sharp teeth; small size.

2. BROAD-FOOTED MOLE, Sca-
panus latimanus; Talpidae,   Mole
Fam. Mouse +. Color silvery-gray to blackish-brown; the ears and

Mead.
Str. Wd.

eyes not visible in thick fur; hunts underground creatures in soil.

3. SHREW-MOLE, Neurotrichus gibbsii. Mouse size; 3-3 1/2"
Mead. long; tail 1 1/2". Unlike the Broad-footed Mole, the front feet are
Str. Wd. longer than broad, the eyes are small but distinctly visible and the
Sub-alp. tail is much more haired; nose naked; color dark brown. In N. Sierra.

4. VAGRANT SHREW, Sorex vagrans; Soricidae, Shrew Fam.
Mouse -; 2-2 1/2"; tail short for a shrew, only 1 1/2"; color grizzled
and dark marked; under parts yellowish-white. Tiny size and long
Mead. pointed nose distinguish shrews from mice. Usually dart about quick-
Str. Wd.
Sub-alp. ly, hunting insects and mice in thick vegetation and debris. Found
from Kern Co. north, but not in north Coast Ranges.

5. ADORNED SHREW, Sorex ornatus. Mouse size; 3 1/4-4 1/4"
Str. Wd. long; tail 1-1 1/2". Grayish-brown to sooty brown above, lightly
Mead.
Sub-alp. marked with silver-tipped hairs; brownish-gray below. W. side mts.

6. YOSEMITE or TROWBRIDGE SHREW, Sorex trowbridgei.
Mead. Mouse -; 2 1/2" long; tail 2" Dull brown above, grayish below; tail
Str. Wd. grayish-brown above and whitish below. Tulare Co. N. at low elev.

7. DUSKY SHREW, Sorex obscurus. Mouse -; 2 1/2-2 3/4". Very
Mead. dark brown above; ashy-gray below; tail black on top, white beneath.
Str. Wd. From San Jacinto Mts. north, but not in N. Coast Ranges.

8. MOUNT LYELL SHREW, Sorex lyelli. Mouse -; 2 1/4-2 1/2"
Sub-alp. long; tail 1 1/2". Brown above; gray below. Rare, in high mts. above
8000', from S.E. Tuolumne Co. to N.W. Fresno Co. Grass or willows.

9. WATER SHREW, Sorex palustris. Mouse size. 3 1/2" long;
Str. Wd.
Water tail 2 1/2". Hind feet very large and tufted with stiff white hairs to aid
in swimming; black upper parts contrast with white belly. Tulare Co. N.

C. Order CHIROPTERA, Bats. Flying Mammals, going south in
winter, or hibernating in caves.

Sub-alp. 10. LITTLE BROWN BAT, Myotis lucifugus; Vespertilionidae,
Rocks Common Bat Fam. Mouse size. Wingspread 10 1/2"; body and head
Water 3 1/2"; color light brown. Like most bats, it catches insects in the
Mead. dusk. This species appears in late summer in high mts., usually
Brush flying high among tree tops. Found from Kern Co. north.
Conif.

11. CALIFORNIA MYOTIS, Myotis californicus. Mouse size or
Str. Wd. -; 3" long; wingspread 9 1/2". Dark ears contrast with bright-yellow-
Mead.
Conif. brown fur, with bases of hairs dark; body paler below; foot 1/2-1/4"
long compared to nearly 1/3" long in #10. Low elev., W. side of mts.

12. LONG-EARED MYOTIS, Myotis evotis. Mouse size; 3-3 1/2"
Conif. long. Golden-brown and glossy fur; large black ears. Often seen
Mead. darting back and forth between high tops of trees at dusk, generally
Rocks in openings in ponderosa pine forest or lower red-fir forest.

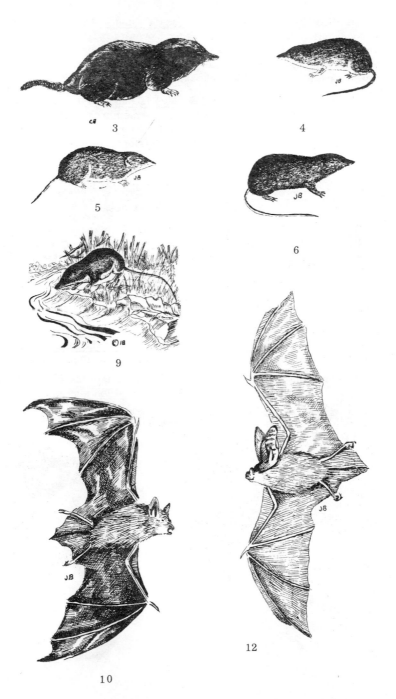

3

4

5

6

9

10

12

13. HAIRY-WINGED MYOTIS, <u>Myotis volans.</u> Mouse size, 3 1/2-4" long; tail 1 1/2-2". Varies from dark brown to yellowish-brown or cinnamon above; wing membranes and ears blackish; ears short; fur on underarm extends out farther than on other Myotis. Found from Nevada and Mendocino Counties south.

Conif.
Mead.
Str. Wd.
Rocks

14. SMALL-FOOTED MYOTIS, <u>Myotis subulatus.</u> Mouse size; 3-3 1/2" long; tail about 1". The black wing membranes and ears contrast with the golden-brown or bright yellowish-brown back; face black. The foot is relatively small, 1/4-3/8"; flat-topped forehead. Found from Tuolumne and Inyo counties south. Ear longer than snout.

Rocks
Conif.
Mead.
Str. Wd.

15. BIG BROWN BAT, <u>Eptesicus fuscus.</u> Mouse +; 4 1/2" long. <u>The only large brown bat</u>; glossy, bright brown fur. Wingspread 13". Nose, feet, wing membranes and ears are black.

Mead.
Str.Wd.
Rocks

16. RED BAT, <u>Lasiurus borealis.</u> Mouse size to Mouse +; 4-4 1/4" long. <u>Yellowish-red fur tipped with white</u>; top of head naked; ears very small. From Shasta Co. south at lower elevations.

Conif.
Str.Wd.

17. HOARY BAT, <u>Lasiurus cinereus.</u> Mouse +; 5-6" long. A <u>large gray bat, the fur sprinkled with black</u> (hoary). Summer visitor, hanging in trees by day. Ears black-bordered.

Conif.

Str.Wd.

18. SILVERY-HAIRED BAT, <u>Lasionycteris noctivagans.</u> Mouse size; 3 3/4-4" long; <u>covered with thick, chocolate-black fur,</u> fringed with silvery white; ears short and rounded. From Plumas Co. N.

Conif.
Water
Str.Wd.

Bats are important in keeping down the number of insects, such as mosquitos. Their very rapid squeaks are often too high to be heard.

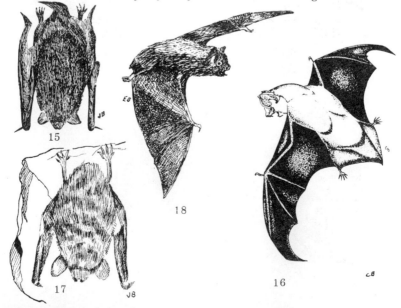

FACE
BROWN

C. Order CARNIVORA, Carnivorous Mammals.

19. BLACK BEAR, Ursus americanus; Ursidae, Bear Fam. About 4-5' long; weight 200-500 lbs. Color tawny, brown or black. An omnivorous feeder, eating everything from acorns to marmots.

Brush
Conif.
Sub-alp.
Mead.
Str.Wd.

20. RACCOON, Procyon lotor; Procyonidae, Coon Fam. (See illustration on p. 41). 2-3' long; color grayish with black markings; stout body. Omnivorous feeder, usually foraging near water.

Str.Wd.
Conif.

21. RING-TAILED CAT, Bassariscus astutus; Bassariscidae, Cacomistle Fam. Cat size; 14-16" long. Hunts mice and rats; eats wild fruit. Light brownish color above, whitish below; ringed tail. A very shy animal of lower and middle altitudes.

Brush
Rocks
Str.Wd.

22. PINE MARTEN, Martes caurina; Mustelidae, Weasel Fam. Cat size; 17". Brown on the back; orange or yellowish tinge to throat and belly; black-tipped, bushy tail. Bounds and bounces along; leaps from branch to branch, chasing after squirrels. From Kern Co. north.

Conif.
Sub-alp.
Mead.
Rocks

23. FISHER, Martes pennanti. Raccoon -; 20-25" long. Black color; slender, powerful body; head may appear grizzled brownish. Savage hunter of smaller life, even martens. From Kern Co. north.

Conif.
Sub-alp.

24. MINK, Mustela vison. Cat size; 12-17" long. All dark brown in color; white chin. Hunts fish, mice, rats, etc. Expert swimmer.

Conif.
Water
Str.Wd.

21

22

23

24

Conif.
Rocks
Mead.
Sub-alp.

25. ERMINE or SHORT-TAILED WEASEL, Mustela erminea. Rat -; 6 1/2" long; tail about one-third of body and head length; under-parts yellowish-white, often brown above; white mark on nose; body turns white in winter. A fierce little hunter of mice. (Not illus.)

Conif.
Sub-alp.
Rocks
Mead.

26. LONG-TAILED WEASEL, Mustela frenata. Rat size; 8-11" long. Underparts yellowish-white, brown above, white mark on nose; very similar to above, but tail about one-half length of head and body together. May become pure white in winter.

Mead.
Sub-alp.

27. BADGER, Taxidea taxus. Raccoon -; 18-22" long. Gray color, white face with black markings; powerful front feet are used for digging out ground squirrels.

Conif.
Sub-alp.
Mead.
Rocks

28. WOLVERINE, Gulo luscus. Raccoon +; 36-40" long. Looks like a small, bushy-tailed, brown bear with a tawny stripe along the side and a yellowish-brown forehead. Feeds on marmots, squirrels, grubs, carrion, etc. Very savage. From Kern Co. N. to Placer Co.

Water
Str.Wd.

29. RIVER OTTER, Lutra canadensis. Raccoon size; 2-3' long. dark brown color; feet webbed and tail tapered for aid in catching fish. From Yosemite north, in or near water. Very playful, affectionate.

Mead.
Str.Wd.
Conif.

30. STRIPED SKUNK , Mephitis mephitis. Cat size; 13-18". Distinctive black and white colors; day and night feeder on mice, insects, berries, etc.; throws powerful scent. Lower elevations.

Brush
Str.Wd.
Conif.

31. SPOTTED SKUNK, Spilogale putorius. Rat +; 9-14" long. As shown; out mainly at night, hunting insects and mice; throws protective bad scent from two glands; often stands on front feet when alarmed.

Brush
Rocks
Str.Wd.

32. GRAY FOX, Urocyon cinereoargenteus; Canidae, Dog & Fox Fam. Raccoon-size; 2-3' long. Grayish in color, with yellowish-red along sides and on legs; a dark stripe down back. Lower altitudes.

Conif.
Sub-alp.
Mead.
Rocks

33. RED FOX, Vulpes fulva. Raccoon size, 2-3'. Usually with yellowish-red fur, though 3 other phases are also found, the cross fox (with dark band on back), and the black and silver foxes. Distinguished by black ear tips, black feet and white-tipped tail.

34

Most
Habitats

Brush
Mead.
Conif.
Rocks

34. COYOTE, Canis latrans. Raccoon +; 2 1/2-3 1/2' long. Grayish-brown in color, or yellowish. Appearing like a sheep dog, but with shy and slinky habits; tail often held between legs, especially when running; feeds on harmful rodents and hares, more rarely on livestock or fawns.

35. BOBCAT or WILDCAT, Lynx rufus; Felidae, Cat Fam. Raccoon size; 2-3'. Gray or tawny, spotted

with brown or black; short tail, tufted ears. Eats small animals.

36. MOUNTAIN LION, Felis concolor. 4-6' long; color brownish gray to reddish-brown, but light tawny below; tail long, black-tipped.

Conif.
Sub-alp.
Mead.
Brush
Rocks

C. Order RODENTIA, Rodents. Animals with two upper and two lower, large, front, gnawing teeth.

Mead.
Rocks
Str.Wd.

37. MARMOT, Marmota flaviventris; Sciuridae, Squirrel Fam. Cat size and +; 17" long; bushy tail 7". Thick body; color yellowish-brown, with shoulder grizzled whitish, sides yellowish. Has shrill whistle when alarmed; takes sun baths on top of boulders; hibernates.

Rocks
Mead.
Sub-alp.

38. BEECHEY or CALIFORNIA GROUND SQUIRREL, Citellus beecheyi. Cat size; 14-20" long. Mottled gray and blackish in color, with gray mantle over the shoulders; tail more bushy than most ground squirrels. Mainly at lower altitudes.

Mead.

39. BELDING GROUND SQUIRREL, Citellus beldingi. Rat - to rat size; 6 1/2-9" long; tail short in proportion to body; light yellowish-brown above, and lighter below. Often sits up very straight, looking like a stake and so called "picket-pin gopher." Has loud, clear whistle. From Fresno Co. north, but not in Coast Ranges.

Conif.
Sub-alp.
Mead.
Rocks

40. GOLDEN-MANTLED GROUND SQUIRREL, Citellus lateralis. Rat -, 7" long. Looks like a large chipmunk, but has a thicker body, dark stripes only on the sides (not on head), and a golden or copper-colored "mantle" over the shoulders; also the tail is shorter in relation to body length. Under parts grayish or whitish. Rarely climbs trees as does a tree squirrel, but hides in holes. From Kern Co. N.

Brush
Conif.

41. SONOMA CHIPMUNK, Eutamias sonomae. Length 5-5 1/2"; tail 3 1/2-4 1/2"; mouse +. Dark reddish-gray in color with dull gray brownish light stripes on outer sides; lower dark stripes on head are reddish-brown; a black blotch appears below the ear. Marin Co. N.

Conif.
Sub-alp.
Rocks

42. LODGEPOLE CHIPMUNK, Eutamias speciosus. Mouse +; about 5" long; tail 2 3/4-4". White stripes on rich, reddish-brown sides, and on dark head. This is the common chipmunk of the west side of the Sierra; it climbs trees when frightened, often high up; likes thick clumps of trees. Not found in Coast Ranges.

Rocks
Alpine
Sub-alp.

43. ALPINE CHIPMUNK, Eutamias alpinus. Mouse size or +; 4-4 1/2". A small, pale brownish-yellow chipmunk, without sharply contrasting stripes, but underside of tail light orange-yellow. Rarely climbs trees. Found along crest of mts., Tulare to Tuolumne Cos.

Sage
Conif.

44. LEAST CHIPMUNK, Eutamias minimus. Mouse +; 4-4 3/4" Dark grayish color with white stripes; tips of ears gray; lemon-yellow under tail. Mainly found in sagebrush east of the Sierra Nevada, but occasionally comes up into Jeffrey pine forest of E. side of mts.

Conif.
Brush
Mead.
Rocks
Str.Wd.

45. LONG-EARED CHIPMUNK, Eutamias quadrimaculatus. Mouse +; 5-5 1/2" long. A large white patch behind ear; ear banded longitudinally in gray, black and brown; otherwise similar to above chipmunks. From Madera Co. north to Plumas Co.

46. MERRIAM CHIPMUNK, <u>Eutamias</u> <u>merriami</u>. Mouse +; 5–
5 1/2". <u>Large gray chipmunk</u>; all the light stripes are gray, while the
dark stripes are brown; tail long and flat with light yellow-brown on
the edges; black spots around eyes. From Tuolumne Co. S.   Brush

47. TOWNSEND CHIPMUNK, <u>Eutamias</u> <u>townsendi</u>. Mouse + 5–
5 1/2" long. A dark stripe through the eye, which turns black behind
the eye; <u>back of ears banded vertically in gray,</u> <u>black and brown;</u> reddish-brown under tail. From Fresno Co. north.   Conif.

48. CHICKAREE or DOUGLAS SQUIRREL, Tamiasciurus douglasii. Rat - or rat size; 8" long; tail about 5". Dark brown color above with reddish tints; black lines on sides contrast markedly with white or yellowish under parts. The high-pitched, indignant chatter of the chickaree is familiar in the forest. Gathers pine and fir cones and nuts to eat or store for winter. From Kern Co. north.

Conif.
Sub-alp.

49. CALIFORNIA GRAY SQUIRREL, Sciurus griseus. Cat size; 16" long; tail longer than body, very large and fluffy. Light gray above, white below. Forages far more on the ground for seeds than does the Chickaree. At lower altitudes on W. side of Sierra Nevada.

Conif.
Str. Wd.

50. FLYING SQUIRREL, Glaucomys sabrinus. Rat -; 6-7" long; tail 5-6". The soft and silky fur is grayish-brown above and white below; the eyes are very large and dark; the tail is flattened and the skin spread between the legs to help the squirrel glide from one tree to another (it does not actually fly). Comes out at night .

Conif.

51. MOUNTAIN POCKET GOPHER, Thomomys monticola; Geomyidae, Gopher Fam. Rat -; 5-7". Brown to grayish in color; black down middle of back and on nose; stout body; front feet strongly developed for digging; has outside cheek pouches; lives mainly underground, and feeds chiefly on tubers. Kern Co. N. at high altitudes.

Sub-alp.
Mead.
Alpine

52. BOTTA POCKET GOPHER, Thomomys bottae. Rat -; 5-7" long. Brown to grayish in color, but usually without strong black markings. Found in much lower meadows than above gopher.

Mead.

53. BEAVER, Castor canadensis; Beaver Fam., Castoridae. Raccoon +; 2 1/2-4' long. Stout, brown body; large, flat, hairless tail; cuts down trees with teeth; builds dams. From Tulare Co. N.

Water
Str. Wd.

54. CALIFORNIA POCKET MOUSE, Perognathus californicus. Heteromyidae, Pocket Mice and Kangeroo Rat Fam. Mouse size; 3 1/2-4 1/4" long; tail 4-5 1/2" long. Has deep, fur-lined cheek pouches on either side of mouth on outside. Brownish-gray above; yellowish-white below; tail dark above, light below, crested on tip; black mark on nose; yellow-brown stripe on side. El Dorado Co. S., low elev.

Brush

55. WHITE-FOOTED or DEER MOUSE, Peromyscus maniculatus. Cricetidae, Native Rat and Mice Fam. Mouse-size; 3-3 1/2" long; tail 2 1/2", furred. The soft, brownish fur, large delicate ears, large bright eyes, and clean habits are distinctive; tail less than 90% of the head and body length. Found in almost all habitats except water.

All
but
water

56. PINYON MOUSE, Peromyscus truei. Mouse size; about 3 1/2-4" long; tail a little over 90% of the head and body length, dark brown above, white below; general color brown to dark brown, but creamy white below. East side of mts. in pinyon-juniper woodland, and higher in edge of Jeffrey Pine Forest.

Pin-Jun.
Conif.

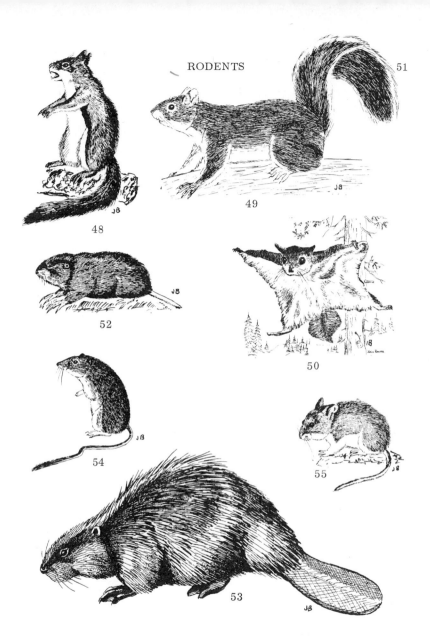

48

49

51

52

50

54

55

53

57. BRUSH MOUSE, <u>Peromys-
cus boylei</u>. Mouse size to mouse +;
3-5" long; <u>tail a little longer than
head and body</u>. Dark brown above
and white below; ears fairly large.
Found mainly at lower elevations.
White-footed mice often come into
abandoned cabins and make their
nests out of mattress stuffings.

56

Brush
Rocks
Conif.
Bldg.

58. WESTERN HARVEST MOUSE, Reithrodontomys megalotis. Mouse size; about 3 1/2"; tail 2 1/2-3". Distinguished by upper incisor teeth being grooved on their outer surfaces. Jumping mice also have such grooves, but their hind legs are large and powerful for jumping. Brownish to blackish above; grayish or grayish-brown below; yellowish-brown sides.

Mead. Conif. Str. Wd. Rocks Brush

59. DUSKY-FOOTED WOODRAT, Neotoma fuscipes. Rat size; 7 1/2-8". Brown above, white below; tail covered with hair; yellowish blotch on belly; tail is round, not flat as in the bushy-tailed woodrat. Often builds large stick nests at lower elevations.

Str. Wd. Conif. Brush

60. BUSHY-TAILED WOODRAT, Neotoma cinerea. Rat size; 9". Grayish-brown color with a squirrel-like, flattened tail; white below; tail covered with hair. Wood rats are sometimes called "trade rats" because they pick up objects and drop others in their place.

Rocks Mead. Conif. Sub-alp.

61. WESTERN RED-BACKED MOUSE, Clethrionomys occidentalis. Mouse size; about 4"; tail about 2" long. Brown mixed with black or chestnut-black above; brownish-gray on sides and below. Found from Plumas Co. N., often in old logs, stumps, in darkest parts of forest.

Conif.

62. MOUNTAIN MEADOW MOUSE, Microtus montanus. Mouse +; 5" long; tail 1 1/2". Dark brown above; light-brown below; thick body, blunt nose, small eyes, tiny ears; often seen running along grassy runways. Found from Tulare Co. N., but not in north Coast Ranges.

Mead. Conif.

63. OREGON or CREEPING MEADOW MOUSE, Microtus oregoni. Mouse size; 3 3/4-4" long; tail 1 1/2-1 3/4". Similar to mt. mouse, but dark brown color above contrasts with grayish below. Found in north Coast Ranges and Mt. Shasta area, then north.

Mead.

64. LONG-TAILED MEADOW MOUSE, Microtus longicaudus. Mouse +; 4 1/2" long; tail 2 1/2". Grayish-brown in color, with grayish-white belly; tail bicolored, dark above, white below. Meadow mice usually have shallow tunnels underground where nests are.

Mead. Sub-alp. Str. Wd.

65. MOUNTAIN LEMMING MOUSE or HEATHER VOLE, Phenacomys intermedius. Mouse +; 5 3/4" long; tail 1 2/5". Color grayer than most meadow mice; does not build runways through the grass, but usually lives near patches of Sierra Heather (see p. 23). Found from Fresno Co. north; rather rare in high meadows.

Sub-alp. Alpine

66. PACIFIC JUMPING MOUSE, Zapus pacificus; Zapodidae, Jumping Mouse Fam. Mouse size; 3 1/2" long; tail 5". The long, scaly and untufted tail plus the very long and strong hind legs are distinctive; body colored reddish-yellow above, brownish down middle of back, and pure white underneath; forelegs weak. Travels by long leaps. From Tulare Co. north, usually in high grass. BIG JUMPING MOUSE, Zapus princeps. Mouse +. Similar to above mouse, but larger and ear bordered with yellow. From Warner Mts.

Mead Sub-alp. Str. Wd.

Mead. Str. Wd.

53

58

59

62

60

64

47.

GOPHER DIGGINGS COMPARED TO THAT OF A MOLE.

66

Mole Hole
Low, fan-shaped mound
of fine dirt deposited at
surface.

Gopher Hole
High, volcano-like mound of
lumpy dirt upheaved from a
tunnel.

See page 41.

See page 50.

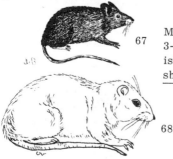

67

68

67. HOUSE MOUSE, Mus musculus, Muridae, Old World Mouse and Rat Fam. 3-4" long; tail 2 3/4-3 3/4"; color grayish or yellowish-brown all over; fur short; tail naked and gray. House pest.

Bldg.

68. NORWAY RAT, Rattus norvegicus. 7-10" long; tail 5-8", naked and scaly. Grayish-brown above; grayish below. A scavenger and pest.

Bldg.
Str. Wd.

69. MOUNTAIN BEAVER, Aplodontia rufa; Aplodontiidae. Mountain Beaver Fam. Rat +; 11-13 1/2" long. Brown marked with white (grizzled) all over; tail often hard to see, 3/4-1 1/2" long; blunt nose and stocky body like meadow mouse, but much larger. A very shy animal of damp, thick vegetation, not at all like true beaver in habits. Found from Tulare Co. north in scattered colonies; a social animal.

Str. Wd.
Conif.
Sub-alp.

70. YELLOW-HAIRED PORCUPINE, Erethizon dorsatum; Erethizontidae, Porcupine Fam. Raccoon size; 18-26" long. Distinctive sharp spines on back and tail; short legs, heavy body; brownish to yellowish-brown body. A dull-witted and slow-moving animal that climbs trees to eat bark and is protected by quills against enemies.

Conif.
Sub-alp.
Str. Wd.

D. Order LAGOMORPHA, Conies and Hares. Four large, front gnawing teeth in upper jaw instead of only two as in rodents.

71. CONY or PIKA, Ochotona princeps; Ochotonidae, Pika Fam. Rat -; 7" long; tail a little over 1/4"; ear 1". Body covered with light gray, soft fur; looks like a round-eared, short-legged rabbit or a guinea pig; gives a queer, ventriloquial call, seeming to come from all directions, sounding like whistled "eeenk-eeenk!" Eats green plants and dries and stores hay in deep nest in rock slide for winter. Found from Tulare Co. north, excepting in Coast Ranges.

Rocks
Mead.
Sub-alp.

72. BLACK-TAILED HARE or JACK RABBIT, Lepus californicus; Leporidae, Rabbit and Hare Fam. Cat +; 16-22" long. Color grayish, with tail black above. Has large ears and powerful hind legs, useful in escaping enemies by running. Lower altitudes.

Brush
Sage
Mead.

73. WHITE-TAILED HARE, Lepus townsendii. Cat +; 18-24" long; tail 3 1/2"; ears 6". In summer it is pale brown with white tail; in winter all white with black-tipped ears. Tulare N. to Lassen Co.

Mead.
Sage
Pin-Jun.

74. SNOWSHOE HARE, Lepus americanus. Small cat size; about 15" long; tail 1-1 3/4"; ears about 3". Very large feet, 4" long, also hairy to aid in walking on snow; color brown in summer, white in winter. From Tuolumne Co. north, especially among willows.

Str. Wd.
Conif.
Sub-alp.

70

69

71

72   73   74

E. Order ARTIODACTYLA, Hoofed Mammals.

75. MULE DEER, <u>Odocoileus hemionus;</u> Cervidae, Deer Fam.
4-5' long.   <u>Color brown, with black-tipped tail</u>; bucks grow new set
of horns each year; fawns dark-spotted on golden-brown.   The deer
of the N.W. Sierra and N. Coast Ranges is called the California Black-
tailed Deer (top tail shown), while the deer of the interior ranges and
the southern California mts. is called the California Mule Deer.

> Conif.
> Sub-alp.
> Mead.
> Brush
> Str. Wd.

76. ELK, <u>Cervus canadensis.</u> 5-6' long, with <u>pale yellow rump;</u>
bull with very large antlers, loud bellowing or squealing challenge in
the fall. General brown color. Scattered in N.W. and near Owens Val.

> Mead.
> Conif.

77. BIGHORN SHEEP, <u>Ovis canadensis</u>; Bovidae, Sheep and Ox
Fam. 3-3 1/2' high, 4' long.   Brown to brownish-gray, with <u>white
rump; large, curved horns in males</u>. Expert rock climber. Go in
small bands, mainly on E. side of Sierra Nevada near Owens Valley.

> Rocks
> Mead.
> Sage
> Pin-Jun.

76

ER

77   75

BIRDS

Because of the wings of birds, they can move about easily from one region to another. So we observe that some are resident all the year, some are winter visitors, others spring and fall migrants. Unless otherwise described, a bird is assumed to be an all year resident.

On account of limited room, the descriptions of birds that follow are very short and cover only the most important characteristics. But every one is pictured and sometimes bird flight patterns or feeding behavior are also shown when these are particularly useful in identification. Sometimes the male (♂) only is pictured since the male is easiest to identify, and the female (♀) is usually found present with the male. Note particularly types of bills (see illustrations), types of feet (also illustrated), sizes and shapes of bodies, and methods of feeding, flying and acting. Where important, these are emphasized by underlining or by arrows. Note also the kinds of habitats or wildlife areas where each kind of bird likes to live.

Nuthatch	Woodpecker	Swallow
Finch	Hawk	Duck
Shorebird	Heron	Merganser

TYPES OF BILLS

Because the pictures of the birds in the pages that follow are not always in proportion to the actual sizes of the different birds described, it is important to have some other method of giving you a proper feeling of size. For this reason five familiar birds are taken as examples of bird sizes. Study their pictures carefully and compare the warbler (4-5") with the sparrow (5-6 1/2"), the robin (8-10"), the pigeon (13-16"), and the crow (18-24"). In the descriptions of birds, the sizes are given in comparison to the five above birds, with a - after the name meaning a little smaller, and a + meaning a little larger than the example. Thus crow + means a little larger than a crow. If you always think of these sizes it will help you.

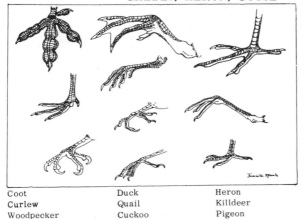

A. Order PODICIPEDI-FORMES, Grebes. Differ from ducks by sharp bill, narrow head and neck (always held erect), poor flight, swift diving, and tailless look. Catch fish, frogs, etc.

Coot	Duck	Heron
Curlew	Quail	Killdeer
Woodpecker	Cuckoo	Pigeon
	Sparrow	

TYPES OF FEET

1. EARED GREBE, <u>Podiceps caspicus</u>. Colymbidae, Grebe Fam. Robin +. In summer the large black crest on head is distinctive; also has brown facial tufts; neck black; back and wings dark. Summer.   Water

2. PIED-BILLED GREBE, <u>Podilymbus podiceps</u>. Robin +. The thick, round bill, marked with black in summer is distinctive. Occasional in summer in lower elevation lakes.   Water

B. Order CICONIFORMES, Herons. Very large birds, curving neck in S-shape when flying. Feed on frogs, mice, fish, etc.

3. GREAT BLUE HERON, <u>Ardea herodia</u>; Heron Fam., <u>Ardeidae</u>. About 4' high. Bluish-gray, with white head & neck & long legs. Sum.   Water Str. Wd. Mead.

C. Order ANSERIFORMES, Ducks, Geese, Swans.
   (1) Family <u>Anatidae</u>, Geese, ducks, etc.
      a. <u>Geese</u>. Larger than ducks; feed mainly on grain.

4. CANADA GOOSE, <u>Branta canadensis</u>. Crow ++; about 40" long. Body gray, head and neck black, with white cheeks. Flock in wedge-shaped flight, with hoarse, honking cries. Tulare Co. N.   Water Mead.

Water

b. <u>Surface-feeding Ducks</u>. These obtain food by dabbling and tipping up the body instead of diving for it. In rising from the water, they spring straight up as shown.

5. GREEN-WINGED TEAL, <u>Anas</u> <u>carolinensis</u>. Pigeon-size; very small and gray for a duck; <u>head of ♂ reddish-brown, with green stripe through eye</u>; the back is gray; wing marked with green.   ♀ duller, speckled. Occasional fall or spring migrant, mainly N. of Lake Tahoe.

Water

6. MALLARD, <u>Anas</u> <u>platyrhynchos</u>. Crow +. <u>The only ♂ duck with green head and neck, reddish-brown breast, and white ring on neck.</u> ♀ brown with orange bill. Usually winter visitor, low elev.

Water

7. SHOVELLER, <u>Spatula</u> <u>clypeata</u>. Crow size. <u>Bill is spoon-shaped</u>; head and neck dark green, sides chestnut, belly white (in ♂); ♀ light brown. Occasional in fall and winter in lower lakes & ponds.

Water
Str. Wd.

8. WOOD DUCK, <u>Aix</u> <u>sponsa</u>. Crow size. ♂ beautifully colored and irridescent in winter and spring with metallic green head crested with violet lined with white; bright red area at base of bill.   ♀ generally brown and white; ♂ similar in summer and fall. Both sexes have nasal "krrr-eeek" call; ♂ has soft, mellow whistle.   Low elev.

c. <u>Diving Ducks</u>. These ducks dive deeply for food.   In rising from the water, they patter along surface, as shown in picture.

Water

9. BUFFLEHEAD, <u>Bucephala</u> <u>albeola</u>. Dove +. <u>♂ very distinctive black and white with puffy-looking head.</u> ♀ much darker, with white mark on cheek. Occasional in summer in high lakes, mainly from Lassen Peak **N.**

d. <u>Mergansers</u> (fish ducks); bills with tooth-like edges.

Water

10. COMMON MERGANSER, <u>Mergus</u> <u>merganser</u>. Crow +. ♂ is black and white; ♀ is grayish with a reddish-brown head and crest. The slender bill with toothed edges is used for catching fish. A line of mergansers often flies over the water so low as to almost touch it. From Tulare Co. north; occasional in summer on streams.

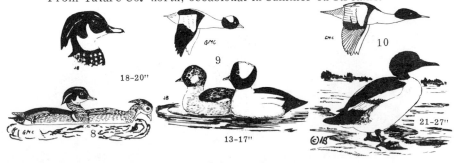

D. Order FALCONIFORMES, Vultures, Hawks, etc.
  (1) Fam. <u>Cathartidae</u>, Vultures. Feed on dead animals.

11. TURKEY VULTURE, <u>Cathartes aura</u>. Crow + +; wing-spread 6'; <u>naked red neck</u>; <u>black general color with 2-toned wings</u>. Summer.

Sub-alp.
Brush
Mead.
Rocks
Conif.

  (2) Fam. <u>Accipitridae</u>, Hawks and Eagles.
    a. <u>Short-winged Hawks</u> (also called Bird Hawks). Distinctive long tails and broad short wings, beaten very rapidly.

12. GOSHAWK, <u>Accipiter gentilis</u>. Crow size or +; wingspread up to 45". This is much the biggest of the three bird hawks; upper parts bluish-gray; <u>light gray underparts</u>. Found from Ken Co. N.

Conif.
Sub-alp.
Mead.

13. COOPER HAWK, <u>Accipiter cooperii</u>. Crow size. <u>Tail rounded, reddish-brown underneath and barred</u>; body bluish-gray. Wingspread 30-35". Fiercely dives at birds through foliage.

Conif.
Sub-alp.
Str. Wd.

14. SHARP-SHINNED HAWK, <u>Accipiter striatus</u>. Pigeon +; wingspread 20-25". Looks like Cooper Hawk, but smaller and has a <u>square tail</u>. Mainly found in mountains in summer.

Conif.
Mead.

b. Buzzard Hawks and Eagles. These birds have very long, broad wings and short, usually broad tails.

Brush
Rocks
Conif.
Sub-alp.
Mead.

15. GOLDEN EAGLE, Aquila chrysaetos. Wingspread 6-8'. From a distance looks dark brown or blackish all over; closer shows golden tints. Soars high in sky, but drops like meteor on prey.

Rocks
Str. Wd.
Conif.
Sub-alp.
Mead.

16. RED-TAILED HAWK, Buteo jamaicensis. Crow size and + wingspread 4-5'. Tail bright red above; thickest body and shortest tail of all Buteo hawks. Cry, a shrill "kreeeeer!" Like most hawks of this type, it does much good by eating harmful rodents and rabbits.

Mead.

17. SWAINSON'S HAWK, Buteo swainsoni. Crow size; wingspread 3-4'. Light wing linings contrast with dark flight feathers; narrow, dark bands seen against light tail. Lower elevations.

c. Harriers. Show long wings and long tails. Harry small animals by chivvying them back and forth till tired.

Lower
Mead.

18. MARSH HAWK or HARRIER, Circus cyaneus. Crow size. ♂ bluish-gray above, with white rump; tail with black bars; throat and breast gray; white belly marked with brown. ♀ brown above, streaked with brown on breast; white rump. Shrill "kek-kik-kik" cry.

(3) Fam. Falconidae, Falcons. Long, pointed wings; all have fairly long tails.

Mead.
Rocks
Conif.
Sub-alp.
Str. Wd.

19. SPARROW HAWK or KESTREL, Falco sparverius. Robin size. Reddish-brown tail and back; yellowish-brown below; often hovers over fields, watching for grasshoppers and mice.

E. Order GALLIFORMES, Grouse and Quail.
    (1) Family Tetraonidae, Grouse.

Conif.
Sub-alp.

20. SOOTY GROUSE, Dendragapus obscurus. Crow - to crow size. About the size and shape of a chicken hen; the long rounded tail is banded with gray at end; body dark gray. ♂ softly hoots.

(2) Fam. Phasianidae, Quail.

Brush
Mead.

21. CALIFORNIA QUAIL, Lophortyx californica. Robin +. Forward curved plume; gray color marked with black and white.

Brush
Conif.
Mead.

22. MOUNTAIN QUAIL, Oreortyx pictus. Pigeon -. Gray body, dark-barred flanks, reddish-brown throat; long, straight plume on head. Loud, resonant "t-woook!" or "t-yoork" cry; "cut-cut" of ♀.

F. Order COLUMBIFORMES, Pigeons and Doves.

Conif.
Mead.
Str. Wd.

23. MOURNING DOVE, Zenaidura macroura; Columbidae, Pigeon and Dove Fam. Pigeon -; 11-13" long. Gray color, pointed tail, soft "coo-coo-cooo!" cry of the ♂ are distinctive; white shows on edge of tail in flight. Found at lower elevations. Summer Vis.

16

red

9–12"

17

19

18

9–11"

10–11 1/2"

22

21

reddish-brown

23

20

Conif.

24. ˈBAND-TAILED PIGEON, Columba fasciata. Crow -. Stout body; broad, dark-banded and rounded tail; yellow legs; bluish-gray back and wings contrast with black tips of wings; white crescent on back of neck of adult; an owl-like "whoo-ooo" call.

G. Order CHARADRIIFORMES, Sandpipers and relatives.
    (1) Fam. Charadriidae, Plovers.

Mead.
Water

25. KILLDEER, Charadrius vociferus. Robin size. Generally with white breast, gray back, tawny rump and tail base, and 2 black breast bands. Shrill "kee-deer" cry; often cries constantly in flight.

(2) Fam. Scolopacidae; Sandpipers.

Mead.
Water

26. COMMON SNIPE, Capella gallinago. Robin +. Yellowish-brown and black stripes on head, and brownish general color, lighter below; very long bill. Zig-zag flight, and raspy cry.

Water
Str. Wd.

27. SPOTTED SANDPIPER, Actitis macularia. Robin -. Brown above, white belly spotted with black; teeters along, bobbing up and down. Summer, in and along streams.

(3) Fam. Larinae, Gulls.

Water

28. CALIFORNIA GULL, Larus californicus. Crow +. General gray color; adult with the under side of wing tipped with straight edge of black; body white below. From Yosemite north on lakes.

Water

29. RING-BILLED GULL, Larus delawarensis. Crow size. A light gray above, yellow legs; a black band around bill. In mt. lakes.

14-16"

24   25   26

6 1/2-8 1/2"

27   28   29

H. Order STRIGIFORMES, Owls.

30. HORNED OWL, <u>Bubo virginianus</u>; Fam. <u>Strigidae,</u> Owls. Crow +. <u>The only large owl with horns, the horns far apart</u>; upper parts dark brown or blackish; under parts light brown and barred. Call, a deep "whoo-hoo-hoo!" Feeds on harmful rodents & rabbits.

Rocks Str. Wd. Conif. Sub-alp. Mead. Brush

31. FLAMMULATED OWL, <u>Otus flammeolus.</u> Sparrow +. Grayish-brown above and whitish below, but marked with black; small ear tufts or horns; a mellow hoot is repeated steadily; very secretive.

Conif.

32. PYGMY OWL, <u>Glaucidium gnoma.</u> Sparrow +. Grayish-brown; tail with white bars; no ear-tufts; <u>black patch back of neck.</u> Call, a monotonous single note or soft whistle, repeated rapidly.

Conif.

33. SAW-WHET OWL, <u>Aegolius acadicus.</u> Robin -. <u>Brown, spotted with white above</u>; no ear tufts; wide, fluffy brown stripes in front; call-note like filing of saw; open wing shows white spots in rows.

Conif. Sub-alp.

34. SPOTTED OWL, <u>Strix occidentalis.</u> Crow size. Head round and without ear tufts; color brown above, but spotted white; <u>light brown below, spotted and barred with white</u>; eyes very large and dark brown instead of the usual yellow. Call, a high-pitched yelping.

Conif.

35. GREAT GRAY OWL, <u>Strix nebulosa.</u> Crow ++; largest of our owls; wingspread of 5'. Dark brown above, marked with grayish-white; light gray breast streaked with dark brown; brown barred gray belly; <u>gray facial disk with brown rings.</u> Deep, echoing "hooo!"

Conif. Sub-alp.

18-25"

30

31

7-7 1/2"

32

JB

33

34

18-19"

25-32"

© IB

35

I. Order CAPRIMULGIFORMES, Night-hawks

**36. COMMON NIGHTHAWK, Chordeiles
minor; Fam. Caprimulgidae.** Robin size.
Mottled brownish color; white bar near dark
wing-tip; flight swift and erratic, high in the
air, in search of insects. Summer.

*Mead.
Conif.
Sub-alp.*

J. Order APODIFORMES, Hummingbirds and Swifts.
(1) Fam. Trochilidae, Hummingbirds.

37. ALLEN'S HUMMINGBIRD, Selasphorus sasin. Warbler -. ♂
with reddish-orange throat, green back, reddish-brown rump; ♀ duller in color, mostly olive-green. ♂ makes U-shaped dive during court-
ship. Occasional in late summer at lower elevations.

*Mead.
Brush*

38. RUFOUS HUMMINGBIRD, Selasphorus rufus. Warbler -. ♂
a rich reddish-brown above; throat coppery-red and shining; a white
band below it; ♀ duller and greenish-olive. Migrant in high meadows.

Mead.

39. BROAD-TAILED HUMMINGBIRD, Selasphorus platycercus.
♂ with green upper parts, whitish under parts and rosy purple throat.
Warbler -. ♀ greenish above, whitish below, with buff on sides. Both
noisy in flight, making constant rattling trill with wings. E. side mts.

*Conif.
Sub-alp.
Mead.*

40. CALLIOPE HUMMINGBIRD, Stellula calliope. Warbler --;
the tiniest bird of the mts. ♂ with upper body golden-green, whitish
below; beautiful lilac-colored feathers radiate out from white throat.
♀ dull olive-green. Females of these 3 hummers look much alike.

*Pin-Jun.
Conif.
Mead.*

greenish   rosy-purple   red   red rays   red   reddish-brown

37   39   40   38

(2) Fam. Apodidae, Swifts. Swifts look like swallows, but
have backward-curving, more pointed wings, are faster, and never
rest on tree tops or telephone wires, but stay high in air; the short
glide & swift, twinkling beat of the stiff wings are also characteristic.

41. WHITE-THROATED SWIFT, Aeronautes saxatalis. Sparrow
+. Sharp black and white colors are distinctive. Summer.

Rocks

42. BLACK SWIFT, Cypseloides niger. Sparrow +. Black color
and slightly-forked tail characteristic. Nests in deep rocky canyons.

*Rocks
Mead.*

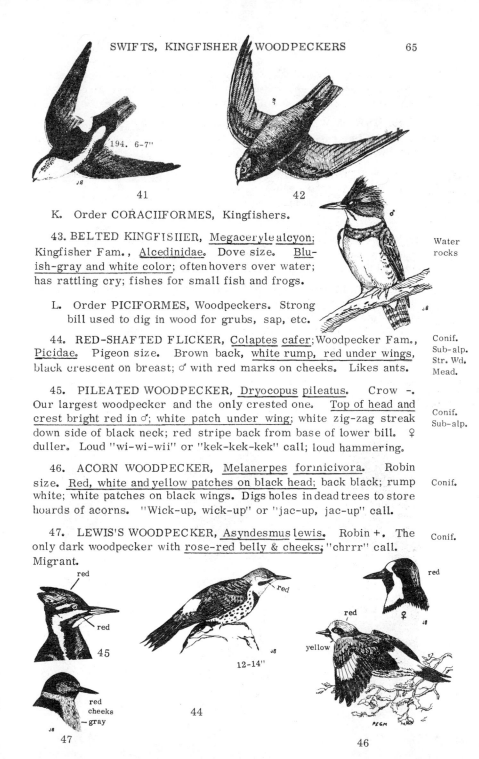

41   42

K. Order CORACIIFORMES, Kingfishers.

43. BELTED KINGFISHER, <u>Megaceryle alcyon</u>;
Kingfisher Fam., <u>Alcedinidae</u>. Dove size. <u>Blu</u>-
<u>ish-gray and white color</u>; often hovers over water;
has rattling cry; fishes for small fish and frogs.

Water
rocks

L. Order PICIFORMES, Woodpeckers. Strong
     bill used to dig in wood for grubs, sap, etc.

44. RED-SHAFTED FLICKER, <u>Colaptes cafer</u>; Woodpecker Fam.,
<u>Picidae</u>. Pigeon size. Brown back, <u>white rump, red under wings</u>,
black crescent on breast; ♂ with red marks on cheeks. Likes ants.

Conif.
Sub-alp.
Str. Wd.
Mead.

45. PILEATED WOODPECKER, <u>Dryocopus pileatus</u>. Crow -.
Our largest woodpecker and the only crested one. <u>Top of head and</u>
<u>crest bright red in ♂; white patch under wing</u>; white zig-zag streak
down side of black neck; red stripe back from base of lower bill. ♀
duller. Loud "wi-wi-wii" or "kek-kek-kek" call; loud hammering.

Conif.
Sub-alp.

46. ACORN WOODPECKER, <u>Melanerpes formicivora</u>. Robin
size. <u>Red, white and yellow patches on black head</u>; back black; rump
white; white patches on black wings. Digs holes in dead trees to store
hoards of acorns. "Wick-up, wick-up" or "jac-up, jac-up" call.

Conif.

47. LEWIS'S WOODPECKER, <u>Asyndesmus lewis</u>. Robin +. The
only dark woodpecker with <u>rose-red belly & cheeks</u>; "chrrr" call.
Migrant.

Conif.

Conif.
Sub-alp.
Str. Wd.

48. HAIRY WOODPECKER, Dendrocopos villosus. Robin size. White back and size are distinctive; red on top of head; black wings marked with white; black tail bordered with white. "Kink" note.

Str. Wd.

49. DOWNY WOODPECKER, Dendrocopos pubescens. Sparrow +. Looks like small edition of Hairy Woodpecker. Low altitudes. A metallic "kink" call; also rapidly descending notes like horse's whinny.

Conif.
Sub-alp.

50. WHITE-HEADED WOODPECKER, Dendrocopos albolarvatus. Robin size. The pure white head and black body are distinctive; red patch on neck; large white wing patches flash in flight. "Wick-wick".

Sub-alp.

51. BLACK-BACKED THREE-TOED WOODPECKER, Picoides arcticus. Robin size. Black above, except for bright yellow patch on head of ♂; barred white and black below; center tail feathers black, outer white. Tears bark. From Tulare Co. N.; not in Coast Ranges.

Sub-alp.
Conif.

52. WILLIAMSON'S SAPSUCKER, Sphyrapicus thyroideus. Robin size. The black back, white shoulder patch and white crown in the ♂ are distinctive; also has narrow red patch on throat and white face stripes. ♀ brownish, with alternating black and whitish-brown bars on wings and sides; yellow belly and white rump. Nasal "wee-er" call.

Conif.
Str. Wd.
Sub-alp.

53. RED-BREASTED or YELLOW-BELLIED SAPSUCKER, Sphyrapicus varius. Robin size. Breast, neck and head bright red; belly yellowish; back and wings striped and spotted white and black. A very secretive bird with soft, nasal-sounding squeal. Summer visitor.

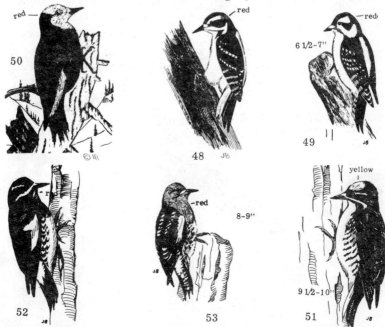

M. Order PASSERIFORMES, Perching Birds.
  (1) Fam. <u>Tyrannidae</u>, Flycatchers. Flycatchers perch quietly
    on branch ends or telephone wires, suddenly circling out to
    snap up insects, then back to the perch again. The first
    four flycatchers listed below (<u>Empidonax</u> sp.) look very
    much alike and are therefore best told apart by habitat and
    song. Carefully check these differences. Summer visitors.

54. WESTERN FLYCATCHER, <u>Empidonax</u> <u>difficilis</u>. Sparrow -.
Throat and rest of under parts yellowish; <u>white eye ring</u> and wing   Str. Wd.
bars; body olive-brown. A monotonous call note, repeated over and
over, wheezy in tone. Perches in shady places 10-30' high. Summer.

55. TRAILL'S FLYCATCHER, <u>Empidonax</u> <u>traillii</u>. Sparrow size.
Similar to above, but less yellowish. Explosive, clear-toned call of   Str. Wd.
"weeps-a-dee-yar!" Hides in dense willow & alder thickets. Summer.

56. HAMMOND'S FLYCATCHER, <u>Empidonax</u> <u>hammondi</u>. Looks   Conif.
like above birds, but habitat very different. Very soft, 3-syllable   Sub-alp.
song, ending with a rising inflection. Usually perches 30' or + high.

57. WRIGHT'S FLYCATCHER, <u>Empidonax</u> <u>wrightii</u>. Sparrow size.
looks like above birds, but habitat different. Song similar to 56's,   Conif.
but louder and more varied, sometimes with 4 notes. Usually seen   Sub-alp.
close to ground in bushes and lower branches of conifers. Summer.

58. WESTERN WOOD PEWEE, <u>Contopus</u> <u>sordidulus</u>. Sparrow   Conif.
size. A plain, dark, gray-brown bird, with <u>no eye-ring</u>, but two   Sub-alp.
white wing bars; call a nasal "pee-wee." Summer visitor.   Str. Wd.

59. OLIVE-SIDED FLYCATCHER, <u>Nuttallornis</u> <u>borealis</u>. Robin   Conif.
-. <u>Distinctive large head and dark chest spots</u>, with white stripe down   Sub-alp.
center of belly; otherwise similar to wood pewee. Loud, ringing call   Str. Wd.
is given from tip-tops of conifers, "pee-pee-paw". Summer visitor.

5-5 1/2" 54   58   59

  (2) Fam. <u>Hirundinidae</u>, Swallows. Wings are characteris-
    tically shaped, not as narrow and stiff as swifts; do not
    appear to twinkle. Hunt insects by swooping low.

60. TREE SWALLOW, <u>Iridoprocne</u> <u>bicolor</u>. Sparrow size. Green   Conif.
or blue-black above and bright white below. Summer visitor.   Str. Wd.
                                          Mead.

Bluish-black

5-5 1/2"

60   61   62

Conif.
Mead.
Brush

61. VIOLET-GREEN SWALLOW, <u>Tachycineta thalassina.</u> Sparrow size. <u>Dark colors contrast with white patches near tail.</u> Summer visitor, nesting in cracks in cliffs. 2-3 "tsee-tseep-tsweet" notes.

Mead.
Conif.

62. PURPLE MARTIN, <u>Progne subis.</u> Robin -. ♂ <u>is blue-black all over;</u> ♀ whitish on the belly. Summer visitor, low elevations.

(3) Fam. <u>Alaudidae,</u> Larks.

Sub-alp.
Alpine

63. HORNED LARK, <u>Eremophila alpestris.</u> Sparrow +. <u>Black collar below yellow throat;</u> streaked brown on upper parts; walks instead of hops. From Nevada Co. to Lassen Co. in high mt. meadows.

(4) Fam. <u>Corvidae,</u> Crows and Jays.

Conif.
Sub-alp.
Str. Wd.

64. STELLER'S JAY, <u>Cyanocitta stelleri.</u> Pigeon size. <u>Dark black and blue, with crest.</u> Has many harsh calls, often given rapidly, and copies scream of red-tailed hawk; also has soft warble.

Pin-Jun.
Conif.

65. PINYON JAY, <u>Gymnorhinus cyanocephala.</u> Robin +. Looks something like a short-tailed, <u>dull blue</u> crow; has no crest. Usually travels in leap-frogging flocks; melodious, mewing call note instead of harsh cries of other jays. Mainly on E. side of Sierra Nevada.

Str. Wd.
Mead.
Conif.

66. CROW, <u>Corvus brachyrhnchos.</u> 17-21" long. <u>All black;</u> voice a harsh caw. Often travels in flocks; found at lower altitudes.

Rocks
Sub-alp.

67. RAVEN, <u>Corvus corax.</u> Crow +. All black, but larger and stouter of body; <u>throat feathers often appear rough or stick out;</u> flies with wings straight out instead of bent up as does a crow. Voice a harsh croak. Nests on cliffs; feeds largely on carrion.

Sub-alp.
Conif.
Alpine

68. CLARK'S NUTCRACKER, <u>Nucifraga columbiana.</u> Pigeon size. <u>Light gray above;</u> <u>black wings marked with white;</u> white tail has central black feathers. A harsh "kraa-aa!" call.

Str. Wd.
Sage
Pin-Jun.
Conif.

69. BLACK-BILLED MAGPIE, <u>Pica pica.</u> Crow -. This is the only bird this side in the Sierra with <u>black and white colors and long, sweeping tail.</u> Staccato "kek-kek-kek" call; also nasal "maagh. " It is found on the lower edges of the middle mountain forests east of the Sierra Nevada crest.

(5) Fam. Paridae, Bush-tits, Chickadees, etc.

70. PLAIN TITMOUSE, Parus inornatus. Sparrow size. Small, gray-brown bird with crest. "Sick-a-dee-dee" call, but soft, melodious song of "sweety-sweety-sweety". Low elevations.

Conif.
Pin-Jun.

71. MOUNTAIN CHICKADEE, Parus gambeli. Warbler size. White cheeks, black cap, black bib and grayish back are distinctive. A very active insect hunter, sometimes hunting upside down. The CHESTNUT-BACKED CHICKADEE, Parus rufescens, with a reddish-brown back, lives in north Coast Ranges. Lisping "see-dee-dee".

Sub-alp.
Conif.

Conif.

72. BUSH-TIT, Psaltriparus minimus. Warbler size. Tiny, gray-backed bird, usually moving in twittering flocks; long tail is characteristic. Late summer at lower altitudes.

Brush
Mead.
Str.Wd.

(6) Fam. Sittidae, Nuthatches. Climb on bark both head up and head down, hunting for insects in cracks.

Conif.
Sub-alp.
73. WHITE-BREASTED NUTHATCH, Sitta carolinensis. Sparrow -. Gray back, black cap, white undersides. Nasal "kyeer-kyeer" call. Found from Kern Co. north.

Sub-alp.
Conif.
74. RED-BREASTED NUTHATCH, Sitta canadensis. Sparrow -. Reddish instead of white below, gray and black above. Both nuthatches have nasal, repetitive calls, but the red-breasted's is more a monotonous "yank-yank". Black stripe through eye; white stripes above eyes.

Conif.
75. PYGMY NUTHATCH, Sitta pygmaea. Warbler size. Tiny size, very short tail and grayish-brown head are distinctive; dark above, light below; back and wings bluish-gray. A shrill, staccato "tee-dee, tee-dee", also weak "ket-ket-ket" call.

(7) Fam. Certhiidae, Creepers.

Conif.
Sub-alp.
76. BROWN CREEPER, Certhia familiaris. Sparrow size. Streaky brown above, whitish below; pale stripes on head and back; tail used in climbing; climbs upward in spiral; flies to bottom of next tree and starts up again. Call, a light "see." Summer visitor.

(8) Fam. Cinclidae, Dippers or Water Ouzels.

Water
77. DIPPER or WATER OUZEL, Cinclus mexicanus. Robin -. Dark gray, cunky body is often dipped up and down. A land bird turned water bird; swims and walks under water. Summer visitor. Has a loud, insistent ""jig-ic, jig-ic" call; loud, clear song.

(9) Fam. Troglodytidae, Wrens. Tails tip up at cocky angle; are flicked about in a characteristic way.

Str. Wd.
Conif.
Sub-alp.
Brush
Bldg.
78. HOUSE WREN, Troglodytes aedon. Warbler size. Gray-brown above with dark markings; has no white marks. Song gurgles and stutters, loud and then softer; many scolding notes. Summer.

Conif.
79. WINTER WREN, Troglodytes troglodytes. Warbler size. A small, dark wren, with very short tail sharply cocked; often bobs body up and down. From Tulare Co. N. to Plumas Co., occasional in sum.

Rocks
Sub-alp.
80. CANYON WREN, Catherpes mexicanus. Sparrow size. Reddish-brown color, especially on belly, but throat white. Song sprays out liquid notes in staccato, then long double notes, ending in a deep "twee-twee-twee!" Moves higher in summer, lower in winter.

Rocks
81. ROCK WREN, Salpinctes obsoletus. Sparrow size. These last 3 wrens all bob up and down. This is a large gray wren, with white or yellowish-tipped tail feathers, and a white streak over the eye.

(10) Fam. Turdidae, Thrushes.

82. ROBIN, Turdus migratorius. 8-11" long. Distinctively red or reddish-brown breast; blackish head and tail; gray back, yellow bill. Summer visitor.

Conif.
Sub-alp.
Mead.
Alpine
Str. Wd.

83. VARIED THRUSH, Ixoreus naevius, Robin size and very similar to robin, but with dark collar across orange-brown breast. Soft "tchook" cry; clear, breezy song. Summer visitor at lower elevations.

Brush

84. HERMIT THRUSH, Hylocichla guttata. Sparrow +.   Brown
back, spotted breast and reddish-brown tail and rump.   A long and
Conif.
Sub-alp. extremely beautiful song, flute-like in quality; "chuk" alarm note; a
nasal "psee" and clear "kee" calls. Summer visitor.

85. RUSSET-BACKED or SWAINSON'S THRUSH, Hylocichla us-
tulata. Sparrow +.   Olive-brown to gray-brown above, without any
Str. Wd. reddish-brown on tail or rump; yellowish-brown ring around eye;
spotted breast.   A soft and beautiful song, gradually spiralling upward in pitch. Summer at lower elevations.

Conif.   **86. WESTERN BLUEBIRD,** Sialia mexicana. Sparrow +. Only
Sub-alp. bird of this size with tail, head and wings blue, while the breast and
Mead.   back are reddish. ♀ brownish, with blue wings and tail. Summer.
Str. Wd.

87. MOUNTAIN BLUEBIRD, Sialia currucoides. Robin -. ♂ sky
Conif. blue all over except for the white belly. ♀ paler, brownish with blue
Sub-alp. on tail region and wings. A simple "cu-cu-cu" song. Summer on E.
Mead.
Alpine   **88. TOWNSEND'S SOLITAIRE,** Myadestes townsendi.   Robin
size, but much more slender. Gray colors, white eye ring, white-
Sub-alp. sided tail, and yellowish spot in center of wing are distinctive.   A
Conif. creaking "eesk" call; a long, warbling song, made while ♂ spirals
into sky, then zig-zags in steep pitches back to earth.

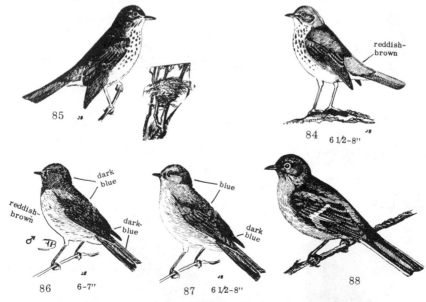

(11) Fam. Sylviidae, Kinglets. Constantly flirt wings.

89. GOLDEN-CROWNED KINGLET, Regulus satrapa. Warbler -.
Conif. Bright orange or yellow crown in ♂; white stripe over eye; grayish-
Sub-alp. green general color. Moves quickly. Thin, hiss-like "see-see" note.

90. RUBY-CROWNED KINGLET, Regulus calendula. Warbler -. Olive-gray above, bright white eye ring; whitish below. A harsh "karr" note, a "chep-chep!" alarm note. Song begins with 2-3 shrill notes, followed by softer phrase, then "ti-dee-dee" repeated.

Conif.
Sub-alp.

(12) Fam. Motacillidae, Pipits.

91. PIPIT, Anthus spiniletta. Sparrow size, but with slender bill, and slender, grayish body; the yellowish underparts are streaked with brownish. Characteristic teetering of tail and walks instead of hops. Found in high meadows, but somewhat rare, and usually in the fall.

Sub-alp.
Mead.
Alpine

(13) Fam. Vireonidae. Vireos. Vireos are often mistaken for small flycatchers or warblers, but they are much duller colored than most warblers, more secretive and slower-moving. They do not take the upright position on a twig as do the flycatchers and have much brighter, more warbling songs; also vireo eye rings look like spectacles.

92. WARBLING VIREO, Vireo gilvus. Sparrow size. A dull, grayish-brown bird, with no distinguishing marks, but a long, slow, warbling song. Low, soft "chu-chuh" note. Summer visitor.

Str. Wd.
Sub-alp.

93. SOLITARY VIREO, Vireo solitarius. Sparrow size. Has bright white wing bars, bright white spectacle-like eye rings and bright white throat; grayish-green above. Short, variable, whistled song; "chee-wee" and "whee-wee" notes. Summer Visitor.

Str. Wd.
Conif.

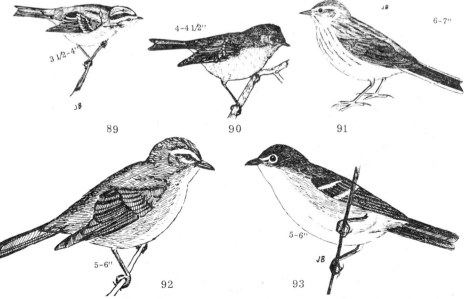

89   90   91

92   93

(14) Fam. Parulidae, Wood Warblers.   Usually brightly-colored birds with thin, short bills; flit about restlessly among twigs.

Str. Wd.   **94. ORANGE CROWNED WARBLER,** <u>Vermivora</u> <u>celata</u>. 4 1/2-5"
Brush   long. The plainest-looking of all the warblers; olive green above, but
Sub-alp. yellowish-green below.   Song a very weak and rapid trill, rising in
Conif.   pitch, then descending, repeated over and over. Summer visitor.

           95. CALAVERAS or NASHVILLE WARBLER, <u>Vermivora</u> <u>rufica-</u>
Conif.   <u>pilla</u>. 4 1/2" long.   A plain, <u>olive-green-backed warbler, but under</u>
Brush   <u>parts bright yellow;</u> a white eye ring and a gray head.   Sharp "tsip"
          call; shrill & rapid song. Summer visitor from Tulare Co. north.

           96. YELLOW WARBLER, <u>Dendroica</u> <u>petechia</u>. 4-5" long. The
Str. Wd. <u>only all-yellow warbler</u>, but with light reddish-brown streaks below.
          Light "see-see-see-tee-see" song; "tsick" call. Summer visitor.

           97. AUDUBON'S WARBLER, <u>Dendroica</u> <u>auduboni</u>.   4 3/4-5 1/2"
          long. <u>General brownish-gray color, with yellow patches on the rump</u>
Sub-alp. <u>and side of breast;</u> ♂ shows yellow crown patch, black breast patch
Conif.   and white wing patches in spring and summer. Often catches insects
          like flycatcher by flying out from twig to catch them. Even monotone
          song of "seet-see-tseet" notes, followed by low-pitched trill.   Soft
          "tseep" call note. Mainly summer visitor.

           98. HERMIT WARBLER, <u>Dendroica</u> <u>occidentalis</u>.   4 1/2" long. ♂
Conif.   <u>with yellow head except black throat</u>; gray back streaked with black;
Sub-alp. white wing bars; usually white outer tail feathers; white belly and
          breast. ♀ duller colored. "Tskk" call; brisk, variable song. Sum.

           99. BLACK-THROATED GRAY WARBLER, <u>Dendroica</u> <u>nigres-</u>
          <u>cens</u>.   4 1/2-5" long.   ♂ <u>gray with black and white striped face and</u>
Conif.   <u>black throat</u>; ♀ with whitish throat.   Variable, wheezy song starts
          with "tzeedle, tzeedle" or "zee-zee, zee-zee" in lazy swing.

yellowish-
green

4-5"

94

yellow

96

4-5"

yellow♂

95

4-5"

yellow

yellow

4 3/4-5 1/2"

♂ Spring
97

4 1/2-5"

98

4 1/2-5"

99

100. MACGILLIVRAY'S WARBLER, <u>Oporornis</u> <u>tolmiei</u>. 4 3/4-5 1/2"
long. ♂ has dark gray hood, covering head and neck, and has white
eye-ring. ♀ with paler hood.   Song, a chant-like rolling whistle;
note, a "tick" or "peet". Very secretive, often jerking tail. Summer.

Brush
Conif.
Sub-alp.
Str. Wd.

101. WILSON'S WARBLER, <u>Wilsonia</u> <u>pusilla</u>.   4 1/2-5" long.
Olive-green above and sharply yellow below; black eye on yellow
face; ♂ has black cap. Song begins with rapid "chit-chit-chit", get-
ting louder and faster; rather rare, hoarse "chup" call note. Sum.

Str. Wd.
Brush
Sub-alp.

   (15) Fam. <u>Ploceidae</u>, Weaver Finches.

102. HOUSE SPARROW, <u>Passer</u> <u>domesticus</u>. 5 1/2-6 1/2". ♂ with
completely black throat, gray on top of head; chestnut patch behind
the eye; brown back streaked with black; white wing bars; rest of upper parts grayish; belly whitish.   ♀ with grayish-brown head; brown
and black streaked back; washed grayish-brown breast.   Has very
coarse, quarrelsome "cheep" note. Resident around buildings.

Bldg.

102   100   101

   (16) Fam. <u>Icteridae</u>, Blackbirds, Orioles, etc.   4-5"

103. BREWER'S BLACKBIRD, <u>Euphagus</u> <u>cyanocephalus</u>. Robin
size. ♂ mostly black with purplish and greenish reflections; eye
white. ♀ brownish. Metallic "teck" note; gurgling, wheezy song.

Conif.
Mead.
Str. Wd.

104. BULLOCK'S ORIOLE, <u>Icterus</u> <u>bullockii</u>. Robin size and -.
♂ with black upper back and top of head, black on the throat, black
line through eye; rest of head and body orange; wings dark with white
patches. ♀ yellowish with gray back and wings. Immature similar to
♀, but has black throat. Sharp "skit" call; variable song. Summer.

Str. Wd.

8-10"
103

7-8 1/2"

104

(17) Fam. Thraupidae, Tanagers.

Conif.
Sub-alp.
105. WESTERN TANAGER, Piranga ludoviciana. Sparrow +. ♂ is only bird with yellow body, black wings and tail, and bright red face; ♀ is much paler, grayish-green above and yellowish below. Soft "pick" note; rising and falling song, like robin's.

(18) Fam. Fringillidae, Finches, Sparrows, etc. All have thick, short bills for seed-eating.
a. Dark Grosbeaks.

Str. Wd.
Conif.
106. BLACK-HEADED GROSBEAK, Pheucticus melanocephalus. Sparrow +. ♂ with black head, reddish-brown breast and black and white wings; a very thick bill. ♀ duller, with striped head. A sharp "pick" call; liquid, mellow song of lifting and falling notes. Summer.

Sub-alp.
Conif.
107. EVENING GROSBEAK, Hesperiphona vespertina. Sparrow +. Stocky body, short tail, thick bill, yellowish general color, black markings and bright white wing patches are distinctive. ♀ brownish-gray with yellowish wash; black wing and tail feathers edged with white. Both sexes have very large greenish-yellow bills. A shrill, chirped "tseer-ip" call; rough "tseereep, greea" song. Scavenger.

b. The Red and Yellow Finches.

Conif.
Str. Wd.
108. CALIFORNIA PURPLE FINCH, Carpodacus purpureus. Sparrow size. ♂ is brown, with rose red on rump, head and breast; whitish below; ♀ grayish-brown with dark streaks on whitish under-parts. Call a sharp "pit!" Song, a staccato, rolling warble. Summer.

Sub-alp.
Conif.
109. CASSIN'S PURPLE FINCH, Carpodacus cassinii. Sparrow size to sparrow +. The rose red of the head on the ♂ sharply contrasts with the brown neck and back, the breast and rump are pale rose color; whitish below. ♀ similar to that of 108. Song like above, but broken into rolling, vibrant warble that ends in "chrrrr!" Startled "stay-dee-yeep!" note of alarm. Summer visitor.

Alpine
110. GRAY-CROWNED ROSY FINCH, Leucosticte tephrocotis. Sparrow size. Body dark brown, touched with pink on the rump and wings; gray on middle and back of head, black on front. ♀ duller. Coarse "cheep, cheep" or "chee-chee-chee" calls.

Sub-alp.
Conif.
111. RED CROSSBILL, Loxia curvirostra. Sparrow size. ♂ is brick red with dusky wings and tail; ♀ greenish-gray with yellowish underparts. Bill strongly crossed for opening pine seeds. Loud "pip-pip" cry; warbled "tu-tee-tu-tee, tu-tay" song.

Sub-alp.
112. PINE GROSBEAK, Pinicola enucleator. Robin size or -. The only very large, reddish-colored finch with white wing bars and gray-black tail. ♀ more grayish-yellow. Deeply notched tail. 2-3 whistled "tee-tee" notes; sharp "preer"; other twitterings and whistles; rich, melodious song. From Tulare Co. to Plumas Co.

bright red

105

108

5-6"

106

107

109

112

gray

pink

brown

110

111

5-6 1/2"

113. **LESSER GOLDFINCH,** Spinus psaltria. Warbler size. The ♂ with greenish back, black cap, black and white wings; yellow below ♀ duller. Sweet, plaintive "tee-yeer" note.
Conif.
Str. Wd.
Mead.

114. **PINE SISKIN,** Spinus pinus. Warbler size. Brown, streaked with yellow. Flies in flocks that often veer from side to side erratically, all twittering at once. Wheezy "kee-see-ee" note.
Conif.
Mead.

c. Towhees and Buntings.

115. **BROWN TOWHEE,** Pipilo fuscus. Robin size. Brown all over, except for rusty-brown rump. Buzzy notes; metallic "tink".
Brush

8-10"

115

4 1/2-5"

114

3 1/2-4"

113

Brush
116. RUFOUS-ṢIDED TOWHEE, Pipilo erythrophthalmus. Robin -. Black above, marked with white, red sides, white belly. Loud "meow"-like note; song a loud, buzzing trill.

Brush
117. GREEN-TAILED TOWHEE, Chlorura chlorura. Sparrow +. Plain olive-green above, grayish below; under surface of wings yellow; sparrow-like bird with reddish-brown crown and bright white throat, bordered with black streaks. Churring song; soft "mew" call.

Brush
118. LAZULI BUNTING, Passerina amoena. Sparrow size. ♂ bright blue above, except for black and white wings, reddish on breast, white belly. ♀ dull brown. Thin, shrill song, starting with 2 notes: "weet-weet" or "hew-hew"; a "tsik" alarm note; ♂ flies high to sing. Tail often jerked nervously.

d. Sparrows.

Conif.
Sub-alp.
Mead.
119. CHIPPING SPARROW, Spizella passerina. 5-5 1/2" long. Gray, plain breast and white line above eye; black line across eye; reddish-brown crown. "Sip" call note. Summer visitor.

Brush
Str. Wd.
120. FOX SPARROW, Passerella iliaca. 6 1/4-7 1/4" long. Very large, dark sparrow; brownish-gray with heavily-streaked breast and belly; reddish-brown tail. Much vigorous scratching under bushes. Song, 2 soft, sweet notes, followed by loud trills; metallic "sisp" note.

Mead.
Sage
121. VESPER SPARROW, Pooecetes gramineus. 5 1/2-6" long. Flashes white outer tail feathers in flight; reddish patch on wing base; body brown above, streaked with dusky. Song starts with 2 clear, flute-like notes, going on to sound like "taps". Mainly E. side mts.

Mead.
Brush
122. WHITE-CROWNED SPARROW, Zonotrichia leucophrys. 5 1/2-7" long. A large brownish-gray and black-backed sparrow with distinctive white and black striped head; breast pearly-gray. Metallic "pink" call; song starts with "saay-see-say", followed by trill.

Sage
Brush
123. SAGE or BELL'S SPARROW, Amphispiza belli. 5-5 1/2" long. Color generally gray; distinctive black marks on sides of the throat and single black spot on breast. Long, square tail often jerked about. A soft "kik-kik" call; a thin, high and jerky song. Summer.

Sage
124. BLACK-THROATED SPARROW, Amphispiza bilineata. Colored gray above; black throat patch, white stripes on the face; whitish below. Immature without head marks. Cheerful "see-see-tsee" or "sweet-sweet-wee" song, ending in a higher or lower trill. Generally found on east side of the Sierra Nevada. Summer visitor.

Mead.
Sub-alp.
125. LINCOLN'S SPARROW, Melospiza lincolnii. 5-6" long. Grayish-brown above, with narrow dark brown markings; the whitish breast finely-streaked with brown. Soft to loud "tsee" or "tsep" call; gurgling song starts with low notes, rises and lowers rapidly, ending softly. Often the song has pauses between phrases.

126. OREGON JUNCO, <u>Junco oreganus</u>. 5-6" long. Reddish-
brown back and black head; tail feathers flash white in flight; buff on
sides; white belly. ♀ grayer on head. Quivering, insect-like trill.
Also twitters and makes clicking noises. Often in large flocks.

Sub-alp.
Conif.
Mead.

reddish

116   7-8 1/2"

117   6 1/4-7"

118

red - brown

119   5-5 1/2"

120

121

124

4 3/4-5 1/4"

123

122   6-7"

125   350. 5-6"

126   5-6"

REPTILES

Reptiles appear mainly during the warm months of the year, going into winter sleep in various hiding places in cold weather. Reptiles have a covering of tough scales that protect them against drying out and against enemies, whereas amphibians, such as frogs and salamanders, have a smooth to warty, moist skin. No native reptiles in California, except the rattlesnakes, are dangerously poisonous. The rest are harmless, usually do lots of good by eating harmful animals and insects, and should be protected.

The reptiles listed below are divided into sections according to types of scales, head shape, etc. When identifying a reptile, carefully study these sections to see into which one it fits. Then see what animals in the section are found in your neighborhood, and study the descriptions and pictures of these to see which one fits your specimen.

A. Order TESTUDINATA, Turtles and Tortoises.

1. PACIFIC POND TURTLE, Clemmys marmorata; Fam. Testudinidae, Common Turtles. About 1' long. Color brownish-yellow, the grayish-brown neck with dark spots. Lives most of time in water, but basks part of time on logs and rocks in sun; feeds on water plants, insects and dead animals. Found at lower elevations.

*Water
Str. Wd.*

B. Order SQUAMATA, Lizards and Snakes.
    (1) Suborder Sauria, Lizards.
        a. Family Iguanidae, Iguanid Lizards. Head usually covered with large scales; belly scales comparatively small, in irregular rows; small pits or pores usually found on the under side of the thigh; skin tough; scales unequal in size.

2. WESTERN FENCE LIZARD, Sceloporus occidentalis. Head and body about 3" long. Gray-brown color with dark markings above; blue blotches on white belly and throat (sometimes lacking in ♀). Scales on back of thigh large, keeled and overlapping.

*Brush
Rocks
Mead.
Bldg.*

3. SAGEBRUSH LIZARD, Sceloporus graciosus. Head and body about 2 1/2" long. Greenish or grayish-brown above, with 6 lengthwise rows of irregular dark spots; under parts whitish, tinged with blue (darker in ♂); scales on back of thigh are small, smooth, granular and not overlapping; orange or rusty colors along sides.

*Conif.
Rocks
Brush
Sage
Sub-alp.*

        b. Fam. Scincidae, Skinks. Body scales are small, circular and smooth, as shown.

4. WESTERN SKINK, Eumeces skiltonianus. Head and body about 3 1/4" long; light brown color, with 2 yellowish to whitish lines down the back; scales in the light lines along sides bordered by a distinct dark margin. Young animals have blue tails. Comes out at dawn or dusk from hiding places under rocks, logs or debris to hunt insects.

*Conif.
Brush
Mead.*

5. **GILBERT'S SKINK, Eumeces gilberti.** Head and body about 2 1/2" long; color as in #4, though adults may have coppery-red heads, and light lines seem to fade in larger specimens; also the scales in the light lines are bordered by an indistinct margin or margin is absent. From Nevada Co. south, usually under rocks, debris, etc. Mead. Conif.

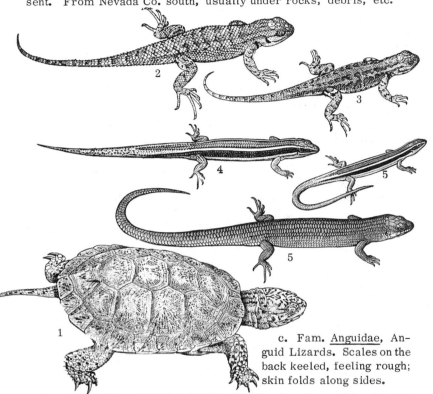

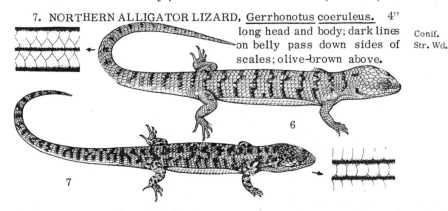

c. Fam. **Anguidae,** Anguid Lizards. Scales on the back keeled, feeling rough; skin folds along sides.

6. **FOOTHILL ALLIGATOR LIZARD, Gerrhonotus multicarinatus.** Head and body about 5 1/4" long; olive-gray to olive-brown on back; dark lines on whitish belly pass down middle of scales (as shown). Conif. Brush

7. **NORTHERN ALLIGATOR LIZARD, Gerrhonotus coeruleus.** 4" long head and body; dark lines on belly pass down sides of scales; olive-brown above. Conif. Str. Wd.

(2) Suborder Serpentes, Snakes. No legs; no eyelids.
    a. Fam. <u>Boidae,</u> Boas and Rubber Boas. Scales under chin
    not elongated, but small or rounded.

8. RUBBER BOA, <u>Charina bottae.</u> Usually under 2' long. Choc-
Conif. olate to dark greenish-brown above, yellowish on belly; the tail very
Str. Wd. blunt, looking a lot like the head; scales small, smooth and skin eas-
ily wrinkled. A secretive snake of damp ground; feeds on mammals.

    b. Fam. <u>Colubridae,</u> Common Snakes. Tail tapers to a
    point; two or more elongated scales under the chin, as
    shown; belly scales more than twice as broad as back
    scales; head scales large; no rattles or poison fangs.

9. SHARP-TAILED SNAKE, <u>Contia tenuis.</u> Rarely more than 14"
long; fairly stout body; <u>tail short, conical and ending in sharp-pointed</u>
Conif. <u>scale</u>; scales smooth, white to cream-colored on belly, generally with
Str. Wd. sharply-marked black borders, giving black and white cross-bar-like
Brush effect; brown, yellowish-brown, reddish-brown or grayish above,
often slightly spotted or marbled with gray-black. Hides in debris.

10. MOUNTAIN KING SNAKE, <u>Lampropeltis zonata.</u> 2-4' long.
Conif. A beautiful snake, banded with red, white or yellowish, and black
Mead. rings; head black above; a gentle, harmless and useful snake. Hunts
Brush lizards, snakes, small rodents, etc. A form lacking red in the colors
is sometimes found around Yosemite Nat. Park. W. of Sierra crest.

Brush 11. COMMON KING SNAKE, <u>Lampropeltis getulus.</u> Usually 2-4'
Mead. long. Banded with black or brown and white. Hunts birds' eggs,
Str. Wd. lizards and snakes, mainly by day; kills by constriction. Low elev.

12. CALIFORNIA STRIPED WHIPSNAKE, <u>Masticophis lateralis.</u>
Brush 2-4' long. A swift and slender snake, grayish-brown in color, with
1 yellow stripe on each side. A good climber in bushes. W. side.

13. DESERT STRIPED WHIPSNAKE, <u>Masticophis taeniatus.</u> 3-5'
long. If scale rows are counted across middle of back, there are 15.
Sage A swift, slender snake, grayish-brown in color like above, but with
Pin-Jun. white stripe on each side generally with a very thin line of black
Conif. (sometimes broken) down its middle; cream to white on belly. Found
along east side of Sierra Nevada at lower elevations. Climbs bushes.

14. WESTERN RING-NECKED SNAKE, <u>Diadophis amabilis.</u> 10-
22" long; with a red or yellowish collar, against a greenish-brown to
Conif. bluish-gray back; head black above; belly red or yellowish. It hides
Str. Wd. by day under rocks, etc.; feeds on worms, insects and salamanders.
Often curls up bright underside of tail to frighten enemies.

15. RACER, <u>Coluber constrictor.</u> 2-4' long. A long, narrow
Mead. snake, colored dark brownish-blue; yellowish on belly; young snakes
Brush are blotched like gopher snake (see below), but scales are not keeled.
This is a fast snake, often catching birds. Low elev. on W. Sierra.

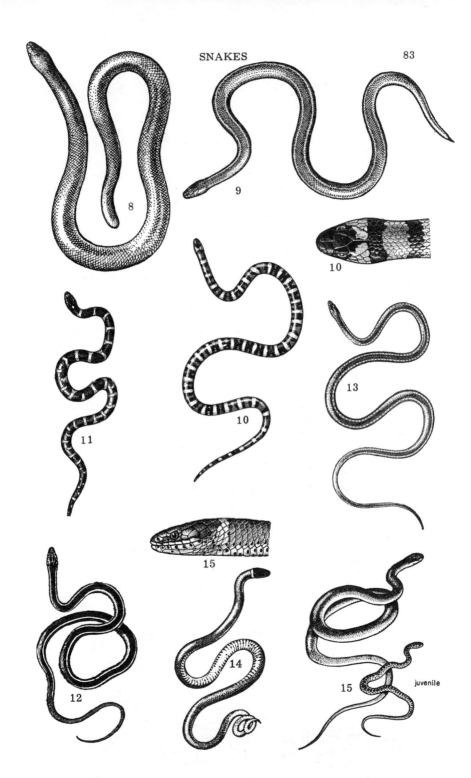

Mead.

16. WESTERN GOPHER SNAKE, <u>Pituophis</u> catenifer. 3-8' long.
Blotched dark brown or black on yellowish-brown body; the scales on
back keeled. Hunts rodents in their holes. Lower elevations.

<u>Garter Snakes have distinctive pungent smell when handled</u>;
back scales keeled.

Mead.
Str. Wd
Water

17. COMMON GARTER SNAKE, <u>Thamnophis</u> sirtalis. 2-3' long.
Grayish-brown in color, with <u>a distinct yellow stripe down middle of
back</u> as well as yellow stripes on sides; <u>usually 7 upper lip scales</u> (as
shown); commonly red-marked between scales. In damp areas.

Str.Wd.
Mead.

Mead.
Str.Wd.
Water

18. WESTERN GARTER SNAKE, <u>Thamnophis elegans</u>. 2-5' long.
Usually with <u>8 upper lip scales</u> (as shown); general grayish-brown
color; red coloring rare. 2 forms: (1) land form (subspecies   <u>ele-
gans</u>) with well-defined yellow back stripe; and (2) water form (subspecies <u>couchi</u>), with a vague to absent back stripe and dark brown
blotches. Most garter snakes hunt lizards, amphibians, fish, insects.

c. Fam. Crotalidae, Rattlesnakes. Head shaped like a blunt
arrowhead; pit behind nostril; rattles at end of tail.

Brush
Rocks
Conif.
Str.Wd.

19. WESTERN RATTLESNAKE, <u>Crotalus viridis</u>. 2-5' long. POI-
SONOUS. Olive-green to gray to gray-brown, <u>with dark brown blotches</u>
<u>bordered by light lines</u>. Hunts small mammals by following body heat.

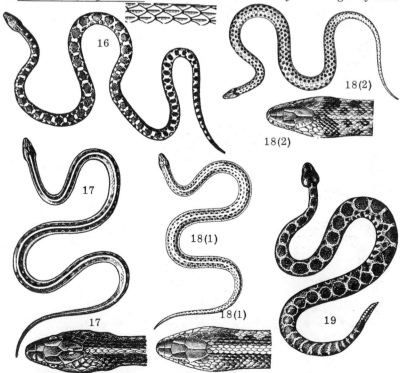

16

18(2)

18(2)

17

18(1)

17

18(1)

19

AMPHIBIANS

Frogs, toads and salamanders appear mainly during damp, mild weather or near permanent water. They have smooth to warty and moist skins. None are poisonous unless eaten. Study the descriptions and pictures for identification of the different species.

A. Order CAUDATA, Salamanders.
  (1) Fam. Salamandridae, Newts and similar forms.

1. ROUGH-SKINNED NEWT, Taricha granulosa. This genus is characterized by uniform dark color above and uniform light color below; also by light silver or yellow patches and a dark horizontal bar in the iris of the eye. 4-7 1/2" long. Usually dark brown or black above, often sharply contrasting with the yellow, orange or red undersides; light color, when present on upper jaw, not reaching the eye; snout blunt. W. slope Sierra from Butte Co. N. and N. Coast Ranges. *Water Conif. Str. Wd.*

2. CALIFORNIA NEWT, Taricha torosa. 6-8" long. Yellowish-brown or dark brown above; usually grades gradually into pale orange or yellow below; light color on upper jaw reached up to the eye; eyes often larger than in 1. Found from El Dorado Co. to Shasta Co. *Water Str. Wd. Conif.*

  (2) Fam. Ambystomidae, Ambystomid Salamanders. Very smooth skins, usually pattern of stripes or spots on back.

3. LONG-TOED SALAMANDER, Ambystoma macrodactylum. 3 1/2-5 1/2" long. Large, prominent eyes; dark brown or black above, with broad light stripe down the middle of the back, though sometimes this is broken into patches; sides and belly white speckled on dark brown or grayish; iris of eye brown flecked with gold. Found from Calaveras Co. N., but not in N. Coast Ranges. Under logs, debris. *Water Conif. Mead. Str. Wd.*

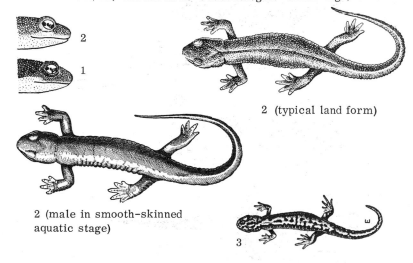

2
1

2 (typical land form)

2 (male in smooth-skinned aquatic stage)

3

Water
Str.Wd.
Conif.

4. PACIFIC GIANT SALAMANDER, <u>Dicamptodon ensatus</u>. Up to 1' long. <u>Stout body with thick limbs;</u> brown to grayish or reddish-brown above, with marbled black or dark brown markings; light brown to cream below, sometimes marked with dark blotches. From Lassen and Lake Cos. north. Has barking call. Near or in streams.

(3) Fam. <u>Plethodontidae,</u> Lungless Salamanders.   Usually smooth-skinned and spotted. Land dwellers; breath by skin.

Str. Wd.
Brush
Conif.

5. CALIFORNIA SLENDER SALAMANDER, <u>Batrachoseps attenua-tus</u>. Head and body 1-2" long. <u>Very slender body and tiny legs characteristic;</u> dark brown to blackish body with light back stripe. Wriggles violently on being discovered. Lake Co. N. and central Sierra.

Rocks
Sub-alp.

6. MOUNT LYELL SALAMANDER, <u>Hydromantes platycephalus</u>. Up to 4 1/2" long. Body and head very flattened; blunt snout; <u>eyes quite small,</u> dark brown or black above, <u>with pale gray to pinkish-yellow mottlings</u> (this color looks like granite rocks); blackish or dark gray below, marked with pale gray. The immature form is usually dark brown or black. From Tulare Co. N. to Tuolumne Co. SHASTA SALAMANDER, <u>H. shastae</u>. Similar to above, but larger eyes, and body and head less flattened. Shasta Co. only. LIMESTONE SALAMANDER, <u>H. brunus</u>. Similar; found in limestone areas of Mariposa County.

Str.Wd.
Conif.

7. ESCHSCHOLTZ'S SALAMANDER, <u>Ensatina eschscholtzii</u>. 3-6" long. Large and prominent eyes; <u>tail smaller at base than immediately beyond, as is shown;</u> color very variable, usually spotted with yellow or white. Found from San Diego Co. north; W. side Sierra.

8. BLACK SALAMANDER, Aneides flavipunctatus. 4-6". Black
or very dark gray above, often spotted or flecked with white or pale
gold; gray-spotted dark gray to black belly. Shasta & Sonoma Cos. N.

Rocks
Conif.

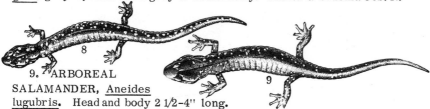

9. ARBOREAL
SALAMANDER, Aneides
lugubris. Head and body 2 1/2-4" long.
Head especially wide behind prominent eyes; dark brown body marked
with yellow spots. Prehensile tail aids climbing. Calaveras-Madera.

Conif.
Brush

B. Order SALIENTIA, Frogs and Toads.
   (1) Fam. Bufonidae, Toads.

Water
Mead.

10. WESTERN TOAD, Bufo boreas. 1 3/4-5" long. Covered with
numerous pale-colored warts; pale stripe down middle of dark back.

Str. Wd.
Conif.

11. YOSEMITE TOAD, Bufo canorus. 1 3/4-3" long. Similar to
above toad, but skin much smoother and more moist, and blotches
on back outlined with fine yellowish lines; belly whitish to yellowish.
♀ and young with contrasting light and dark colors. Madera-Alpine Cos.

Mead.
Sub-alp
Water

(2) Fam. Pelobatidae, Spadefoot Toads. Inner edge of hind foot
with single black tubercle with cutting edge, as shown.

12. INTERMOUNTAIN SPADEFOOT TOAD, Scaphiopus in-
termontanus. 1 1/2-2 1/2" long. Large, protuberant eyes; body
of many colors, from dark green to yellowish to dark brown, usually
with one long, pale-colored stripe down each side. Burrows in the
ground during the day, coming out at night. From Tulare Co. north.

Mead.
Brush
Water

(3) Fam. Hylidae, Tree-frogs. Toe-tips enlarged into suction
discs for aid in agile climbing of rocks and trees.

Water
Conif.

13. PACIFIC TREE FROG, Hyla regilla. 1-2" long; can change
color to that of leaf or bark. Black stripe from nose through the eye.

Str. Wd.
Rocks
Sub-alp.

14. CANYON TREE-FROG, Hyla arenicolor. 1 1/2-2 1/4" long.
Looks like above frog, but skin rougher and no eye stripe. Found
from Kern Co. south, usually in rather arid canyons.

Rocks
Str. Wd.

(4) Fam. Ranidae, True Frogs. No suction cups on toes.

Water
Brush

15A. YELLOW-LEGGED FROG, Rana boylei. 2-3 1/2" long. Inside
of hind leg colored yellow; dark mottled body above, whitish or yellowish below; skin covered with numerous and definite small bumps.
At lower elevations than Sierra Frog. B. SIERRA FROG, Rana mus-
cosa. 2-3" long. Similar to above, but more yellowish on belly, and
less numerous or definite bumps on skin. From Tulare-Plumas Cos.

Water
Str. Wd.
Mead.

Water   16. RED-LEGGED FROG, Rana aurora. 2 1/2-5" long. Inside of
Str. Wd. hind leg colored red; dark mottled above, usually with a dark brown
Mead.   to black mask over eyes. At lower altitudes on W. side of Sierra.

          17. LEOPARD FROG, Rana pipiens. 2-4 1/4" long. Brownish to
Water   greenish or gray above, with large, round, dark spots, finely out-
Mead.   lined with lighter color; light line along upper jaw; yellowish-white
          on belly. Found at Lake Tahoe and a few other high mt. lakes to N.

          18. BULLFROG, Rana catesbeiana. 7-8" long. Very large,
          greenish to black frog, whitish below, with the ear-drums as large
Water   as the eyes. Eats large insects, other frogs and mice. The famous
          and deep bass "jug-o-rum!" call is heard from ♂ at night. Introduced.

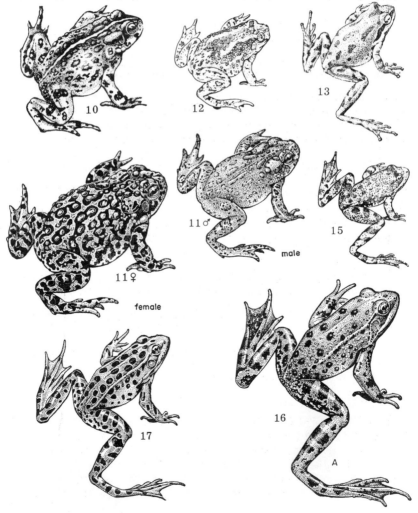

10

12

13

11 ♀
female

11 ♂
male

15

17

16

A

FISH

Wonderful sport fishing is to be had in the Sierras in the clear mountain streams and lakes, but there are also many other interesting fish to be seen in these waters and some are shown here. Before looking at the descriptions of the different fish, study carefully the drawing of a generalized fish below so you will understand the names of the different parts of the body. In naming a fish, make sure it is very close to the description given in this book. Sometimes you will catch or see a rare fish not described here. Because so many kinds of fish have been brought in from outside the state or transplanted within the state, the picture is rather confusing. For this reason, specific ranges for the fish are not given in every case, and fish that have been imported are marked with an asterisk (*).

(NOTE: part of the descriptions below are simplified, with the kind permission of the author and publishers, from A Key to the Fishes of the Sacramento-San Joaquin Basin, by Garth Murphy, published in Volume 27, Number 3, California Fish and Game, July, 1941. The generalized fish picture and the two pictures of parts of fish are also taken, with permission, from the key.)

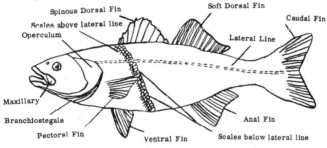

PARTS OF A FISH

A. Fam. Salmonidae, Salmon and Trout. These fish are characterized by having an adipose (or flesh-like) fin on the rear of the back, while the main dorsal fin is shorter than the head and has less than 15 rays. Ventral fins are always on the middle of the body, never just below the pectoral fin. Swift game fish.

*1. BROWN TROUT, Salmo trutta. Usually under 14" long. Dorsal fin with black spots; a few red or brown spots on sides; back with brown spots; ground color above yellowish or greenish-brown, undersides silvery.

1

2. GOLDEN TROUT, Salmo aquabonita. Usually under 14" long. The most beautiful trout of the Sierra; golden-yellow in color, marked with brilliant red, including scarlet stripe on side; olive color on the back; has a thick, rosy, lateral band, marked with dark blotches; lower fins red; scales small. In lakes.

3. RAINBOW TROUT and STEELHEAD, Salmo gairdnerii. Generally under 20" long. Olive-green on back; rose band along middle of sides; dark spots on light background; dorsal fin black spotted. Though they look very similar, the steelhead is partly a salt water fish, while the rainbow stays in fresh water. Belly silvery. Streams.

*4. CUTTHROAT TROUT, Salmo clarkii. Ordinarily 1-15" long. Back is bluish; sides and belly silvery; a red or pink streak on each side of lower jaw; dorsal rays 9-11, generally 10; dorsal and caudal fins covered with many dark spots, as is also most of the body.

*5. EASTERN BROOK TROUT, Salvelinus frontinalis. 7-12"; back mottled with olive and black; front edges of lower fins white; scales very tiny; light spots on dark background; usually red spots on sides. Mainly in streams.

6. LAKE TROUT, Salvelinus namaycush. May reach length of 3' and weigh over 80 pounds. A variable light gray to almost black color, stippled with numerous light spots; tail fin deeply forked; belly silvery, but sometimes lightly spotted. Lakes, especially Tahoe.

B. Fam. Ictaluridae, Catfish and Bullheads. Body without scales; conspicuous barbels or hair-like protuberances around mouth.

*7. SQUARE-TAILED CATFISH or BROWN BULLHEAD, Ictalurus nebulosus. Usually under 18" long. Dark yellowish-brown or blackish in color; fin rays and membranes brown; caudal fin cut off square; large spine in the pectoral fin. Generally in large rivers, up to 6000'. *BLACK BULLHEAD, Ictalurus melas. Very similar, but tail fin not cut off so square, and pectoral spine more weakly barbed.

8. FORK-TAILED CATFISH, Ictalurus catus. Up to 2' long. Similar coloring to the above fish, but more silvery below and more bluish above; caudal fin deeply forked; anal fin with 19-23 rays.

C. Fam. Catostomidae, Suckers. Down-pointing, sucker-like mouth. Generally slow plant feeders along the bottom.

9. SACRAMENTO LARGE-SCALED SUCKER, Catostomus occidentalis; Usually under 18" long; gray-brown above, white below; lateral line scales around 75; 12-14 dorsal rays. Lower streams.

10. TAHOE SUCKER, Catostomus tahoensis. Under 24" long. Lateral line scales 83-92. Found in Lake Tahoe and in streams entering Great Basin; introduced in Feather, Rubicon Rivers, etc.

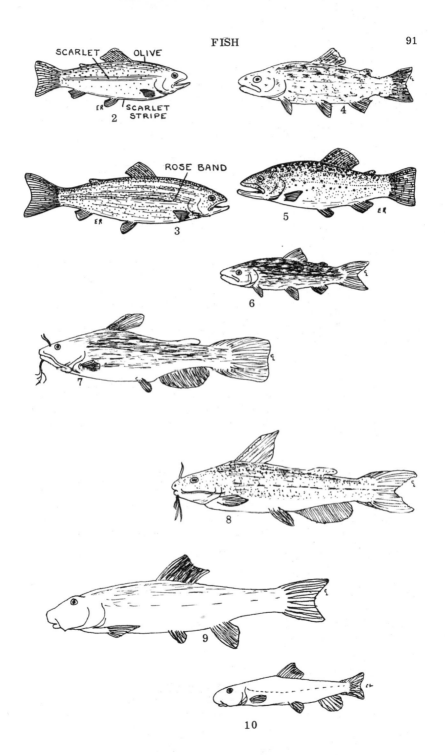

SCARLET OLIVE

SCARLET STRIPE

ER 2

ROSE BAND

ER 3

4

5 ER

6

7

8

9

10

11. LAHONTAN MOUNTAIN SUCKER, Pantosteus lahontan. Under 20" long; similar in color to 9, but shape different (as shown). Found in streams entering Great Basin, and N. Fork Feather River.

D. Fam. Cyprinidae, Carps and Minnows. Dorsal fin completely divided into 2 different portions, one spiny and one soft-rayed.

12. SACRAMENTO SQUAWFISH, Ptychocheilus grandis. Usually under 2' long; greenish-gray color; maxillary near front edge of eye.

13. SPECKLED DACE, Rhinichthys osculus. Length about 4". Premaxillary usually connected to snout by a hidden bridge of fleshy tissue across the groove. There is a thread-like structure (barbel) at the end of the maxillary. Widespread on both sides of Sierra.

14. LAHONTAN REDSIDE, Richardsonius egregia. Up to 11+" long; bluish-gray general color, but bright red sides; golden belly most of year, but red in spring ♂; 2 dark lateral bands on either side of red streak. Found in streams that flow into the Great Basin.

15. TUI CHUB, Siphateles bicolor. Up to 7-8" long. Olive-gray on back, lighter gray below with a dusky lateral band; front of dorsal fin directly over front of pelvic fins; 26-33 scales before dorsal fin.

16. SACRAMENTO WESTERN ROACH, Hesperoleucus symmetricus. Dusky above, pale below, with a partial lateral band. Up to 5" long. Front of dorsal fin is far behind front of pelvic fins; and 32-38 scales in front of dorsal fin. In Sacramento & San Joaquin drainages.

D. Fam. Centrarchidae, Bass and Sunfish.

17. LARGE-MOUTHED BLACK BASS, Micropterus salmoides. Usually under 20". Brownish-green above, only slightly lighter below, thus dark all over and with no narrow stripes; dorsal fins united by a membrane; the anal and soft dorsal fins with no membrane or scales near the base. Found at lower elevations in W. rivers.

18. SMALL-MOUTHED BLACK BASS, Micropterus dolomieu. Usually under 16" long. Golden-greenish colored to dark green; mouth small and not reaching beyond the eye as in the Large Mouth; also has no deep notch in dorsal fin. In large west-slope rivers.

*19. STRIPED BASS, Roccus saxatilis. Usually under 20" long. Body more slender than most bass; with very narrow, longitudinal stripes; two separate dorsal fins; a beautiful and light, bluish-purple in color. Found in larger streams of west slope below 6000'.

20. GREEN SUNFISH, Lepomis cyanellus. Up to 12" long. The anal fin spines are 3; dorsal fin spines 9-11; maxillary reaching just beyond middle of eye; green-brown back; yellow belly. In rivers W.

Crappies (wave-like marks) and Bluegill (orange throat) are also occasionally found in the larger rivers. All are good to eat.

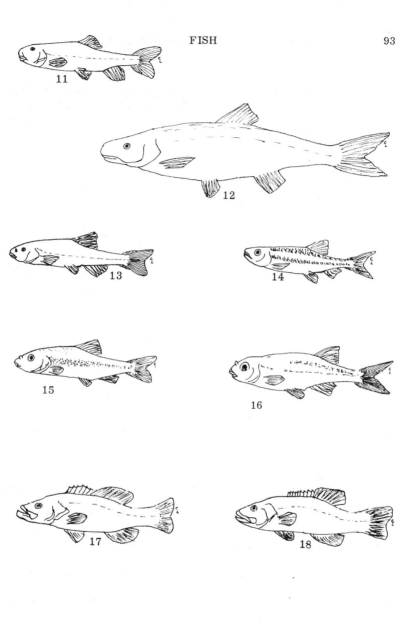

11

12

13

14

15

16

17

18

19

20

94   FISH AND SUGGESTED REFERENCES

E. Fam. Cottidae, Sculpins, Muddlers, etc.

21. PIUTE SCULPIN, Cottus beldingii. Up to 4" long. Grayish,
and mottled in color; hind nostril not tubular; one large spine present
on front edge of gills, no other smaller spines below.   Found in
streams draining into the Great Basin.

22. RIFFLE SCULPIN, Cottus gulosus.   Up to 6-7" long.   The
lateral line is not complete, but extends only to a place below   the
middle of soft dorsal fin.   Dark brown to grayish olive and mottled
over most of body. Found over most of Sierra Nevada.

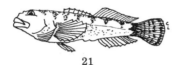

21

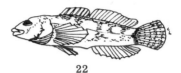

22

SUGGESTED REFERENCES

Abrams, Leroy. Illustrated Flora of the Pacific States, 4 volumes.
Stanford University Press, 1940, 1960.
Brown, Vinson, and Henry Weston, Jr. Handbook of California Birds.
Naturegraph Co. , 1961.
Burt, W. H. and R. P. Grossenheider.   A Field Guide to the Mam-
mals. Houghton, Mifflin Co. , 1952.
Eddy, Samuel. How to Know the Freshwater Fishes. W. C. Brown,
and Co. 1957
Evermann, Barton W. Fishes of Yosemite National Park. San Fran-
cisco Museum, Calif. Acad. of Sciences, 1937, pages 183-201.
Ingles, Lloyd G. Mammals of California and its Coastal waters, Re-
vised Edit. , 1957. Stanford University Press.
Munz, Phillip, and David Keck. A California Flora.   University of
California Press, 1959.
Peterson, Roger T.   A Field Guide to Western Birds, Revised Edi-
tion. Houghton, Mifflin Co. , 1961.
Savage, Jay. An Illustrated Key to the Lizards, Snakes and Turtles
of the West, Revised Edition.   Naturegraph Co. , 1959.
Stebbins, Robert C. Amphibians and Reptiles of Western North Am-
erica. McGraw-Hill Book Co. 1954
Summer, Lowell and Joseph Dixon. Birds and Mammals of the Sierra
Nevada. University of California Press, 1953
Wetmore, Alexander, et. al.   Check List of North American Birds.
American Ornithologists' Union, 1957.

We wish to express our grateful appreciation for the help received from the following individuals and companies: to Dr. M. R. Brittan, Dr. J. H. Severaid and Dr. H. W. Wiedman of Sacramento State College, who gave assistance with the fishes, birds, mammals, and plants respectively; to McGraw-Hill Book Co. of New York City for their kind permission to use the reptile and amphibian pictures of Dr. Robert Stebbins, reproduced in his book on <u>Amphibians and Reptiles of Western North America;</u> to the University of California Press at Berkeley, California, for their permission to use the drawings of amphibians by Dr. Stebbins, originally reproduced in their book on <u>Amphibians of Western North America;</u> and to our artists for their careful work to make this book useful. Major illustrators are listed on page 3. Dr. A. Starker Leopold of the University of California kindly gave his permission to use some of the illustrations by Gene M. Christman (marked GMC in text) from his book, <u>Game Birds and Mammals of California</u> (published by U.C. Student's Store). Other drawings in the book have the following initials: DGK = Don G. Kelley, JGI = James Gordon Irving, PGM = Patritia and George Mattson, MY = Margaret Yarwood, ED = Elizabeth Dasmann, CB = Clyde Burns; BJ = Barbara Johnson, RH = Rosinda Holmes, and JS = Juanita Storch.

INDEX